Listening to the Displaced:
Action Research in
the Conflict Zones of Sri Lanka

Kerry Demusz

First published by Oxfam GB in 2000

© Oxfam GB 2000

ISBN 0 85598 437 6

A catalogue record for this publication is available from the British Library.

All rights reserved. Reproduction, copy, transmission, or translation of any part of this publication may be made only under the following conditions:

- With the prior written permission of the publisher; or
- With a licence from the Copyright Licensing Agency Ltd., 90 Tottenham Court Road, London W1P 9HE, UK, or from another national licensing agency; or
- For quotation in a review of the work; or
- Under the terms set out below.

This publication is copyright, but may be reproduced by any method without fee for teaching purposes, but not for resale. Formal permission is required for all such uses, but normally will be granted immediately. For copying in any other circumstances, or for re-use in other publications, or for translation or adaptation, prior written permission must be obtained from the publisher, and a fee may be payable.

Available from the following agents:
USA: Stylus Publishing LLC, PO Box 605, Herndon, VA 20172-0605, USA
tel: +1 (0)703 661 1581; fax: + 1(0)703 661 1547; email: styluspub@aol.com
Canada: Fernwood Books Ltd, PO Box 9409, Stn. 'A', Halifax, N.S. B3K 5S3, Canada
tel: +1 (0)902 422 3302; fax: +1 (0)902 422 3179; e-mail: fernwood@istar.ca
India: Maya Publishers Pvt Ltd, 113-B, Shapur Jat, New Delhi-110049, India
tel: +91 (0)11 649 4850; fax: +91 (0)11 649 1039; email: surit@del2.vsnl.net.in
K Krishnamurthy, 23 Thanikachalan Road, Madras 600017, India
tel: +91 (0)44 434 4519; fax: +91 (0)44 434 2009; email: ksm@md2.vsnl.net.in
South Africa, Zimbabwe, Botswana, Lesotho, Namibia, Swaziland: David Philip Publishers, PO Box 23408, Claremont 7735, South Africa
tel: +27 (0)21 64 4136; fax: +27(0)21 64 3358; email: dppsales@iafrica.com
Tanzania: Mkuki na Nyota Publishers, PO Box 4246, Dar es Salaam, Tanzania
tel/fax: +255 (0)51 180479, email: mkuki@ud.co.tz
Australia: Bush Books, PO Box 1958, Gosford, NSW 2250, Australia
tel: +61 (0)2 043 233 274; fax: +61 (0)2 092 122 468, email: bushbook@ozemail.com.au

Rest of the world: contact Oxfam Publishing, 274 Banbury Road, Oxford OX2 7DZ, UK.
tel. +44 (0)1865 311 311; fax +44 (0)1865 313 925; email publish@oxfam.org.uk

Typeset by Garth Stewart; printed by Oxfam Print Unit
Published by Oxfam GB

Oxfam GB is a registered charity, no. 202 918, and is a member of Oxfam International.

Contents

Acknowledgements 5

List of abbreviations 6

Introduction 7

1 A history of ethnic conflict in Sri Lanka 8
Political background 9
The context of humanitarian relief 10

2 Why listen to the displaced? 15
Hearing the displaced in emergencies 15
Why is this research important? 16
Objectives of the research, 1996–1998 18

3 How to listen to the displaced: methodology 21
How to listen: early days 22
How to listen: later days 24
How to collect the information 24
Which method to choose? 29

4 Things to consider when researching displacement 31
Training 31
Working with children 33
Gender and women's voices 34
Listening to the disabled 35
Choosing the research participants 35
Selecting the research team 37

5 Analysis 39
Participative feedback sessions 39
Thoughts about analysis 42

6 Outcomes 43
Relief items 43
Gender issues 44
Coping mechanisms 44
People's capacities 45
Past interventions 45
Future interventions 46
Information for advocacy 46

7 Lessons learned 48
Strengths of the methodology 48
Weaknesses of the methodology 49
Looking to the future – next steps 50
Conclusion 52

Notes 53

References 56

Appendices
Appendix 1: How to obtain copies of the research reports 58
Appendix 2: Questions asked in interview groups in 1997 59
Appendix 3: Site Information Recording Sheet 61

Maps
Map 1: Region of the conflict: Sri Lanka / India 8
Map 2: Sri Lanka: nine provinces and 24 districts 10
Map 3: The Wanni and Jaffna 12

Figures
Figure 1: 'Listening to the Displaced' cycle 21
Figure 2: 'Listening to the Displaced' process (detail) 25
Figure 3: Recording the information 28
Figure 4: Collating the information 41

Tables
Table 1: Significant events in Sri Lanka, 1948–1999 11
Table 2: Relief goods test results, 1996 22
Table 3: Samples of focus-group questions, 1997 23
Table 4: Key questions reviewed in 1998 27
Table 5: Facilitation: key issues 31

Index 66

Acknowledgements

My biggest vote of thanks goes to the people working on Oxfam's Sri Lanka programme who made it possible for me to find the time to write this paper. Thanks also to the representatives of Save the Children's Sri Lanka programme who agreed to my writing up this project even though it has become jointly conducted research.

More individually, thanks to Dieneke van der Wijk, who worked with me as the other research coordinator in 1998 and inspired many of the creative ideas on this project. The readers, Allison Aldred, Chris Daniell, Fiona Gell, Simon Harris, and Pauline McKeown, all provided essential feedback and ideas. Catherine Robinson was the first person to inspire and encourage me to write this working paper. Thanks are due also to the Oxfam staff who developed and worked on Listening to the Displaced in the early stages. On a more personal level, thanks to the field staff of both Oxfam and SCF in the Wanni and Jaffna, who continue to work in difficult circumstances in support of poor and marginalised people. Thanks are due also to the financial sponsors of Oxfam GB in Sri Lanka, both Oxfam's general supporters and the Department for International Development (DFID), which provides additional funding.

List of abbreviations

AGA	Assistant Government Agent (head of a sub-District)	LTD	Listening to the Displaced
CARE	CARE International in Sri Lanka	LTR	Listening to the Returned
FORUT	Norwegian acronym for the Campaign for Solidarity and Development	LTTE	Liberation Tigers of Tamil Eelam
		MOD	Sri Lankan Ministry of Defence
		MSF	Médecins sans Frontières
		NFRI	non-food relief item
GA	Government Agent (head of a District)	Oxfam	Oxfam GB Sri Lanka Programme
GS	Grama Sevaka (head of a number of villages)	PLA	participatory learning and action
		POP	people-oriented planning
INGO	international non-government organisation	PRA	participatory rural appraisal
		SCF	Save the Children Fund (UK) Sri Lanka Programme
ICRC	International Committee of the Red Cross		
		SLA	Sri Lankan Army
IDPs	internally displaced persons	UNHCR	United Nations High Commissioner for Refugees
LNGO	local non-government organisation		

Introduction

More and more civilians are affected by armed conflict as the number of local wars around the world increases. With improved worldwide communications, there is more information about natural disasters and their effects on local populations. We hear about these wars and disasters on radio, read about them on the Internet and in newspapers, and see images of them on television. Aid workers, government officials, UN personnel, and journalists tell us about these catastrophes and their practical responses to them — but where are the voices of those directly affected? Where are the voices of the refugees, the displaced, the mothers and the children who have to live in a world torn apart by conflict or natural disaster?

It is that question that this Oxfam Working Paper attempts to answer, with an account of a research project conducted annually by the Sri Lanka programme of Oxfam GB. Called 'Listening to the Displaced' (LTD), the project attempts to enable national authorities and the international community to hear the voices of people displaced by the conflict in northern Sri Lanka. The paper explains the concepts and rationale behind the study, describes the methodology, and discusses how such a listening exercise can be carried out in the context of a civil conflict.

A project like 'Listening to the Displaced' could be implemented by humanitarian agencies as part of an assessment of the needs of people who have been displaced by conflict or natural disaster. It is a useful methodology for listening to people before planning a response that will be relevant to their real needs. This type of project could also be used as a tool to review or evaluate a programme of assistance for displaced people or refugees. In Sri Lanka it has informed programme design as well as advocacy work on issues such as the composition of relief packages and the entitlements of displaced people. A 'listening' project could be used by relief agencies to help them to engage with any population undergoing change resulting from conflict, natural disaster, or economic disaster, including communities who have not had to move, such as host communities or conflict-affected communities *in situ*.

While most relief and development workers in the field actually 'listen' every day, we are often listening with a particular objective in mind, to refine a specific programme or respond to a particular situation. We rarely have the opportunity to listen more comprehensively to a general description of a situation. If we do listen to the expression of broader concerns, we usually record what we have heard only within our own agency reports. A project like Listening to the Displaced helps us to look at a situation holistically, to hear actual voices and let those voices guide our work. A 'listening' project also provides a vehicle for sharing this information with others outside our agencies.

This paper will outline some of the political history and social background that led to the initiation of the 'Listening to the Displaced' project in Sri Lanka. It will explain the researchers' objectives during the first three years of the project, before describing the methodologies employed. Then it will describe how the data were analysed and report what the project has uncovered during the research.[1] Finally, the paper will consider the lessons already learned and look to the future of the project in Sri Lanka.

It is important to remember that Listening to the Displaced is an on-going project in the context of Oxfam's whole programme of work in Sri Lanka. Staff are committed to using research as one means of understanding the ways in which poverty is reinforced by conflict. Listening to the Displaced, in attempting to record the course of displacement and people's experiences of it, is one part of Oxfam's investigation of this process.

1 A history of ethnic conflict in Sri Lanka

Map 1: Region of the conflict: Sri Lanka / India

Political background

Sri Lanka, a small island off the south-eastern coast of India, is perhaps best known as an exporter of tea, or as an international holiday destination. Unfortunately, it is also host to a brutal conflict[2] between the majority Sinhala and minority Tamil populations. Although complex in nature, the conflict can be said in simple terms to arise largely from contested access to services, land, and control of political and administrative power. These tensions have a long history, dating back to the period of British colonial rule, continuing through the period of independence, and finding expression in a violent civil conflict that has persisted for more than twenty years.

Most historians agree that the seeds of the conflict were planted in the early 1900s, when colonial rule did little to promote a sense of national identification among the three main ethnic groups on the island: Sinhala (mostly Buddhist, constituting 74 per cent of the present population), Tamils (mostly Hindus, 19 per cent of the national population), and Muslims (7 per cent). Instead, ethnic and especially regional identification was seen as the primary means of self-identification. This did not necessarily mean that these ethnic groups saw themselves as homogeneous. Indeed, both Tamil and Sinhala groups have always exhibited strong regional affiliations. The **'Sri Lanka Tamils'** (Jaffna Tamils, Colombo Tamils, and Eastern Tamils, originating 2000 years ago from South India, and together constituting 12 per cent of the total population today) and **'Plantation Tamils'** (descendants of Tamils taken from India by the British to work on tea plantations in the nineteenth century, and now forming 7 per cent of the current population) have developed separate regional identities, with sub-groupings within each group according to caste, education, and socio-economic standing. Lowland and highland (Kandyan) differentiation demarcated two important Sinhalese groups, which could be further divided into separate sub-groups. These sub-groupings and the regionalised nature of ethnic groups did little during colonial times or early independent rule to forge a sense of national coherence.

Early disagreements between Sinhala and Tamil groups centred on political representation, the colonisation of traditionally Tamil areas by Sinhala groups (pre- and post-independence), language, and access to employment opportunities and education. In the immediate post-independence period, the new government withdrew citizenship rights for Plantation (Indian) Tamils living in the Central Highlands. A year later, Indian Tamils' voting rights, which they had enjoyed for 20 years, were withdrawn. This set the tone for the post-independence government's interactions with the Tamil population. The early 1970s was an especially difficult time: Sinhala was named as the official language of the administration and the courts, thereby disadvantaging the Tamil population, who held a large proportion of public administration positions; 'standardisation', otherwise known as the university quota system, which reduced the number of Tamils gaining university admission, was brought into effect; in 1972 Ceylon was renamed Sri Lanka, and Buddhism was given special protection under the constitution as the primary religion in Sri Lanka. During this time, the combined effect of these proclamations and laws, and the increasing oppression of the Tamils led to the formation of the first militant groups; one of these was the Liberation Tigers of Tamil Eelam (LTTE).

In 1983 there were island-wide anti-Tamil riots after 13 Sri Lankan Army (SLA) soldiers were ambushed and murdered by a Tamil militant group in Palaly on the Jaffna Peninsula. Thousands of Tamils were killed by Sinhala mobs in the capital Colombo and elsewhere on the island, and hundreds of thousands were displaced. Initially, the authorities did little to stop the mob violence. Since then, the Tamils' militant position has solidified and there has been ongoing active conflict.

The government of India entered the conflict in the late 1980s after the first peace negotiations between the Sinhalese and the Tamils broke down. At the request of the Sri Lankan government, the Indian Peace Keeping Force (IPKF) occupied the northern part of the country in an attempt to 'hold the peace' between the Sinhala and Tamil groups and enforce the Indo-Sri Lanka accord. Within a short time, however, the Tamils and Sinhalese were actually working together covertly to expel the Indians from Sri Lanka. The Tamil groups (especially the LTTE) inflicted heavy losses on the IPKF, which began to withdraw two years later. During this same period, 1988–89, poor, disenfranchised Sinhala youth began a short-lived insurrection in the south of the island. As a result, the entire island was embroiled in violent conflict.

Listening to the Displaced

Map 2: Sri Lanka: Nine provinces and 24 districts

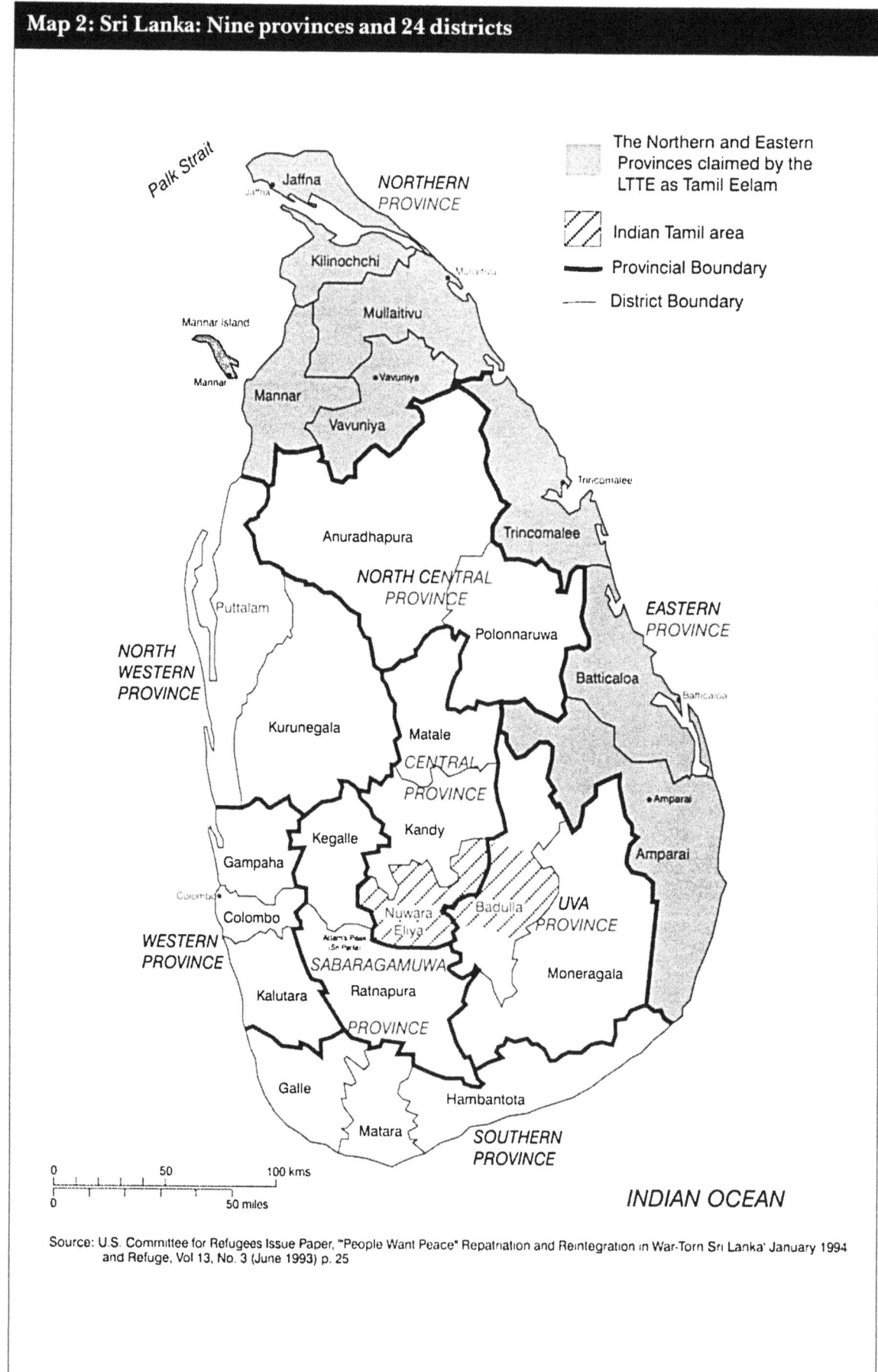

Source: U.S. Committee for Refugees Issue Paper, "People Want Peace" Repatriation and Reintegration in War-Torn Sri Lanka' January 1994 and Refuge, Vol 13, No. 3 (June 1993) p. 25

Violence continued between Tamil groups and the SLA throughout the early 1990s. In the north and east, there were retaliation killings of military personnel and civilians, consolidation of LTTE-held territory — including the expulsion of all Muslims from LTTE-controlled areas in the north – and little political will to bring about change. In 1994, Chandrika Kumaratunge was elected President on a peace platform, and for the first time in years serious peace negotiations were held between the LTTE and the government,[3] but these quickly broke down. The resumption of hostilities has marked a period of massive displacement of the Tamil population and increased militarisation.

The numbers of internally displaced people in Sri Lanka have fluctuated but have been as high as one million: 5 per cent of the population. There are currently an estimated 500,000 internally displaced people, predominantly in the north and east of the island. There are a further 66,000 refugees living in camps in Tamil Nadu, India, and an estimated 35,000–40,000 Sri Lankan Tamils living outside the camps in India. These numbers do not include the people who have sought asylum in and migrated to other countries (see Fuglerud 1999). Nor do they include large numbers of migrant workers now in the Middle East who left the country to find work and who send remittances to their families in Sri Lanka.

What is most disheartening about the current situation is the weak public demand for peace. Pro-peace groups and groups of mothers of soldiers missing in action get little or no press coverage. In 1998, a major military battle for Kilinochchi town resulted in the deaths of more than 1,500 soldiers in a two-day period, but it was barely mentioned in the international media and was censored from the Sri Lankan news. Since 1983, an estimated 50,000 people have died as a result of the conflict, but attempts to negotiate a peace settlement between the two factions have been unsuccessful. In the major urban centres of central and southern Sri Lanka — Colombo, Kandy and Galle — most residents live normal lives unaffected by war. This difference in the daily reality of those living in the centre, outside the conflict area, and those living on the peripheries of the country means that there has been little popular political pressure for peace.

The context of humanitarian relief

In late 1995, the SLA took control of the Jaffna Peninsula and there was a massive displacement of Tamils south from Jaffna into the Wanni region of northern Sri Lanka. 'The Wanni' refers to the geographical area from the central northern town of Vavuniya up to the town of Kilinochchi and the entire territory east to west in between. It comprises most of the four administrative districts of Kilinochchi, Mullaitivu, Mannar, and Vavuniya. However, some of this territory is currently in the 'uncleared area': territory controlled by the LTTE.[4] Estimates at the time suggested that between 400,000 and 500,000 Tamils had moved into a former agricultural region which lacked infrastructure, government services, and funding. A number of people were eventually resettled in rural 'resettlement sites' or went to stay with friends and relatives. To help displaced Tamils cope with this situation, a large humanitarian relief operation was put into action, involving CARE, FORUT, ICRC, Oxfam GB, MSF France and Holland, SCF (Save the Children Fund), and UNHCR. The humanitarian relief effort included the provision of safe drinking water, emergency support for government health services, non-food relief items such as buckets, mats, sheets, clothing and cooking utensils, shelter materials such as plastic sheeting, cadjan — coconut-frond thatching — poles and bricks for single-family home construction, and community health-education initiatives. The Sri Lankan government provided the basic food ration, basic health care, and education services to these internally displaced people (IDPs).

Oxfam has been funding project partners in Sri Lanka since 1969. However, it was not until 1986 that a country office was opened to support partners and to work more closely with communities affected by the escalating conflict. In 1987, Oxfam opened a sub-office in the northern city of Kilinochchi to help build sustainable livelihoods for the population in this impoverished area and to assist those who had been displaced by the serious civil unrest in the central part of the island in 1977 and 1983. This sub-office has been displaced within the north three times, but continues to work with Tamil civilians affected by the conflict. It provides water and sanitation facilities, supports government-sponsored health programmes and works with local partners to give support to a range of economic, psycho-social, and community programmes.

Listening to the Displaced

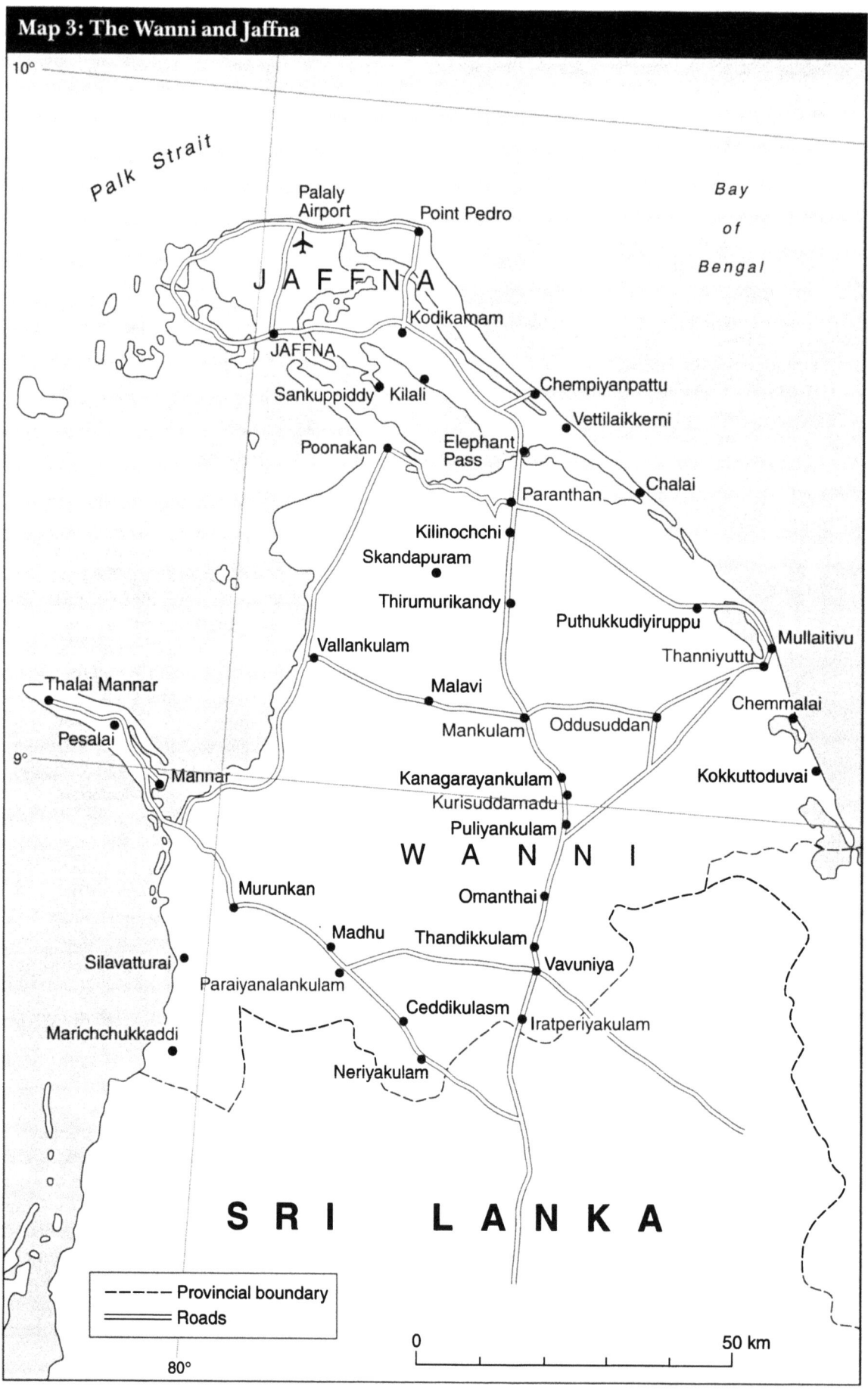

Map 3: The Wanni and Jaffna

Table 1: Significant events in Sri Lanka, 1948–1999

Year	Event
1948	Independence from Britain for Ceylon. Ceylon Citizenship Act denies citizenship to one million 'Indian/Plantation' Tamils.
1949	Ceylon Elections Amendment deprives 'Indian/Plantation' Tamils of voting rights.
1956	Official Language Act makes Sinhala the sole official language of the state.
1958	Sinhalese nationalists force abrogation of proposed Bandaranaike–Chelvanayagam pact to devolve power to regional councils. Non-violent Tamil protests intensify.
1959	Secessionist Tamil uprisings culminate in assassination of Prime Minister Bandaranaike. His widow takes over and continues to promote Sinhalese interests.
1972	Name changed to Sri Lanka. New constitution gives prime place in national life to Buddhism, and defines Sinhala as the official language of the courts and administration. 'Standardisation' of university entrance introduces quotas that discriminate against Tamils. Increasingly militant demands for a separate Tamil state.
1972–78	Emergency rule
1976	Liberation Tigers of Tamil Eelam (LTTE) formed.
1977	Mob violence against Indian/Plantation Tamils in the central highlands causes Tamil exodus to India and the north and east.
1981	Historic Tamil Public Library burns down in Jaffna after political and army violence.
1982	Prevention of Terrorism Act becomes permanent law.
1983	Island-wide anti-Tamil riots kill thousands of Tamils and cause massive displacement after murder of 13 SLA soldiers in Jaffna.
1985	First attempt at Indian-mediated peace talks between Sri Lankan officials and Tamil groups.
1987	Indian Peace Keeping Force (IPKF) lands in Jaffna to enforce Indo-Sri Lankan Accord. Beginning of Eelam War II between LTTE and IPKF.
1988	IPKF occupy north and east of Sri Lanka. Premadasa elected President on promise to send IPKF home.
1989	Sri Lankan government and the LTTE agree a ceasefire; IPKF begins to withdraw.
1990	IPKF withdrawal is completed, but relations between the LTTE and Government break down. Hostilities resume.
1991	Rajiv Gandhi assassinated in Chennai (Madras) by LTTE cadre; deterioration in relations with India.
1994	Chandrika Kumaratunge elected President on a peace platform; first serious peace negotiations between LTTE and government begin. No agreement is reached, and Eelam War III is declared by LTTE.
1995	In November, the SLA takes the Jaffna Peninsula. More than 400,000 Tamils are displaced into the Wanni.
1996	Operation Unceasing Waves I. LTTE regain control of Mullaitivu port, with heavy army casualties. Kilinochchi Town in the Wanni captured by the SLA. More than 100,000 people displaced.
1997	Operation Edi Bala. SLA takes control of the Vavuniya–Mannar road and launches Operation Jaya Sikuru to take control of the Vavuniya–Kilinochchi road. Thousands displaced away from roads as the SLA moves north from Vavuniya.
1998	Operation Unceasing Waves II. LTTE regain control of Kilinochchi town, with heavy military losses on both sides. No displacement. Operation Jaya Sikuru is called off.
1999	Operation Ranagosa I, II, III, and IV. Army takes control of all of Vavuniya District and most of Mannar District. Thousands of families displaced and humanitarian relief supplies delayed. No indication of peace talks. Later in the year the LTTE stages a comeback and recaptures large parts of Vavuniya District.

The humanitarian relief effort in the north and east is undertaken in unusual circumstances, with strict rules governing the way in which aid can be distributed. The Sri Lankan government maintains a civil administrative structure throughout the island, even in the areas controlled by the LTTE where Tamils staff the government positions. Government structures are, however, frequently under-staffed and humanitarian relief efforts are coordinated through these existing (weakened) government structures. While this might have been a positive attribute to the relief effort, in practice it does not help the coordination efforts, because the government representatives in the Wanni are always overworked. These officials are under a great deal of pressure — from the LTTE to 'provide' for the Tamil people and from the government to provide a 'neutral' government service. Under the circumstances, it is impossible to do either.

At the same time, all items being transported into the LTTE-controlled areas need a permit from the Sri Lankan Ministry of Defence (MOD). Indeed, all humanitarian assistance provided by international agencies, the UN, and *even the civil administration* requires this special type of permission; but, because nearly all relief items are considered potentially strategic items, permits are difficult to acquire. Although the MOD tends to allow more permits just after a major victory — such as the taking of the Jaffna peninsula — it is always difficult for aid agencies and government officers to obtain humanitarian relief items and administrative equipment such as paper, fuel, communications apparatus, or vehicles. Access to and from the LTTE-controlled areas is also strictly controlled and limited to the staff of humanitarian agencies and senior government officials with MOD travel permission.

'We don't lead a life. Three years of displacement looks like 35 years; young people look very old now'
(man in Mannar District, 1998)

Postal systems still run in the Wanni, but there are no civilian telecommunication facilities. Government schools and hospitals still function, although at a much-reduced rate of efficacy. Banking facilities still operate, although the government does not permit the transfer of cash to the Wanni. Items that are not part of the ration supplied by the government or are not part of quotas allowed to the Multi-Purpose Cooperative Societies are allowed to enter the Wanni only singly or in small quantities, hand-carried by traders. No electrical or mechanical equipment is allowed into the Wanni without an MOD permit. Fuel and even spare parts for bicycles are severely restricted. There is a thriving black market in restricted materials smuggled in from India or by boat from other parts of the island, but few residents are wealthy enough to afford the exorbitant prices.

The Sri Lankan government and the LTTE see international humanitarian relief agencies as necessary, though both have been known to threaten agencies with expulsion. In the LTTE-controlled areas the presence of international aid agencies offers some protection for civilians and provides them with services. While this continues, the LTTE do not have to devote resources to these areas. The international presence also 'legitimises' the Sri Lankan government's claim of allowing humanitarian aid to its own (Tamil) people, even when relief supplies and food are not allowed into the area for extended periods of time. International humanitarian relief agencies often tread a tenuous line between the two authorities in order to stay and assist a vulnerable civilian population.

2 Why listen to the displaced?

Hearing the displaced in emergencies

The relief operation mounted in Sri Lanka for the displaced from Jaffna focused on technical interventions and a programme that was provided *for* people rather than *with* people. This is characteristic of many emergency programmes, where the priority is on life-saving measures and large-scale response, and where top-down solutions are imposed — rather than using a participatory approach. Few of the better tools that have been developed seem to have been adapted for use in an emergency response — UNHCR's People Oriented Planning (POP) and Participatory Rural Appraisal (PRA) / Participatory Learning and Action (PLA) techniques. Most of these require serious and lengthy consideration of the community structure and cultural patterns, including the division of labour. What the IDPs need or want is often unclear, and their voices are lost in the process. Assumptions about people's basic needs are made so that services can be set up. This process frequently continues even after the emergency is over and the situation has settled. Indeed, the process of 'helping' people can become a difficult habit to break. In addition, when field personnel work within a specific context every day, they feel that they are in touch with the IDPs' needs, even when these 'needs' have not been discussed with the 'needy' for some time.

Another problem that emerges in emergency situations is that agencies focus on dealing with the problem that has been assigned to them or is within their area of expertise, while those affected by the conflict or natural disaster experience a number of problems simultaneously. For example, one agency may assist with safe drinking water, but if no food is provided from any other source, this will do little to solve people's overall problems. There needs to be a better way of understanding how people prioritise their overall needs in such situations, and how to react to those priorities.

These factors led Oxfam to devise a mechanism that would provide a rapid means of finding out what people needed, of ascertaining the social and political trends, and of giving the displaced an opportunity to be heard amidst the chaos of the immediate emergency. At the same time, a method was needed to explore the diversity of the displaced population by gender and by age, so that the perspectives of the different groups in the IDP population could be assessed. Oxfam conducted the first LTD research exercise with people in Kilinochchi District, in January 1996.

This research was repeated and expanded in 1997 and again in 1998. While the actual structure of the reports and the specific objectives of the work have changed over time, the context of the reports remains the same. LTD has attempted to enable the voices of a group of marginalised people to be heard. It has also tried to collect information that can be used for advocacy to uphold the rights of the displaced, focusing on relief and other issues of priority for the displaced community. LTD has tried to look beyond the immediate relief needs of the displaced groups to examine their local capacities and coping mechanisms, as a way to inform programme design. An attempt has also been made to look at the situation in the Wanni over time, by making an effort to return to the same locations each year to track the trends of needs in the north of Sri Lanka.

LTD has always been considered to be 'action research', because its purpose has been to effect change. It reflects the ideas expressed by Burkey (1993):

Participatory action research is the first step in a process of consciousness awakening or conscientisation of the people through their own analysis of and reflection on the causes of poverty and on the socio-economic structures and processes which affect their lives. No development activity can be successful until this process is well underway.

In this way, LTD can serve both as a beginning of the awakening process and the initial construction of a bridge between relief and development. Humanitarian relief operations have been working in Sri Lanka since the early

1980s, and their involvement has waxed and waned with the intensity of the conflict. All of them aim to relieve the distress caused by displacement and the conflict, but they sometimes have difficulty differentiating between relief and development needs. The LTD project was developed to provide information for programmes that provide relief, those that straddle the relief-to-development continuum, and those that are trying to 'do' development or rehabilitation work in conflict situations. It also functions as a tool for enabling voices to be heard even when relief is the major need.

This research project has involved different actors over time. In 1997, Save the Children (SCF) joined the project, participating in the data collection of the 1997 Oxfam survey and then conducting its own initial LTD survey in its area of programme operations. SCF has now become a major partner in the research. This is an ideal situation, because it strengthens the resolve of both agencies to act upon the results of the research. It also constructs a joint position on at least some of the humanitarian issues and provides common ground for advocacy.

A large part of the LTD project is focused on ideas similar to those of Slim and Thompson (1993):

The inclusion of direct testimony in the development debate can help to make it less of a monologue and more of a dialogue ... it is not enough for the development 'expert' to summarise and interpret the views of others — the others must be allowed to speak for themselves.

Why is this research important?

Over the years of this research project, a number of colleagues from other agencies have asked, 'Shouldn't you listen to the displaced every day — rather than once per year?' The obvious answer to this question is 'of course', but while listening every day gives the aid workers, government officials, or whoever may be involved on the ground an understanding of the specific context, not everyone is in a position to listen every day. In addition, donors, the military, and the central government are often not able to hear the displaced people's voices at all. And finally, there are few instances where information is recorded so that it is accessible to others. In this overall context, there are a number of reasons why this research is so important.

For donors, senior government officials, and policy makers

These people are not usually in the field and have little access to the IDPs to whom their funds and services go. In Sri Lanka, the attitude of government officials is often 'We know what the people need', and this type of research can provide them with useful data to inform their decisions. The only other available sources of information are the international agencies, government representatives working in the area, or representatives of the parties to the conflict. The voice of the IDPs has not been heard at all.

The results of the 1998 LTD research, for example, enabled Oxfam and SCF to discuss, with their major donor, a programmatic change away from relief efforts towards promoting self-sustainability. This discussion was actually initiated by the IDP research participants, who expressed needs which Oxfam and SCF in turn expressed to their donor. The IDPs thereby played a direct role in determining the focus of the programmes and how money would be spent.

For local non-government organisations (LNGOs)

Many LNGOs were formed in response to pressure from international NGOs (INGOs) for a mechanism to distribute relief or rehabilitation funds, and to increase capacity to undertake projects, rather than arising from grassroots interest. As a result, much LNGO work is focused on 'projects', which are seen as discrete pieces of work, rather than programmes in which people participate in their own self-defined development. LNGOs in the Wanni also tend to be heavily influenced by, and in some cases controlled by, the LTTE. This means that their links to the communities are often rather weak. What would normally serve as a key source of information about the status of the IDPs is therefore not always an impartial, objective and accurate resource.

One of the uses of LTD is to encourage LNGOs to see people's situation more realistically. The research and the resulting report can often function as a source of information for lobbying LNGOs to act in the people's interests. It can also be used as a training tool with LNGOs to build an understanding of what it means to take people's opinions into account and to work with and for people. This is essential in a situation where local information is at a premium.

For the general public

Access to the LTTE-controlled areas is open only to Tamils, so the remaining 81 per cent of the national population have no first-hand experience of their situation. Even access by humanitarian organisations is very limited. While Jaffna District is marginally more open, very few Sinhala or Muslim civilians actually go there. This sometimes results in populations on both sides of the divide having very serious misconceptions about one another. The small numbers of aid workers, government officials, and traders who do travel back and forth regularly can undo some of these misconceptions; detailed documents from sources not party to the conflict can add to increased understanding between these groups.

Media coverage of the war and the civilian situation is limited, because reporters are not allowed into the LTTE-controlled areas of the north. In Sri Lanka, reports on the conflict area are also censored. Humanitarian agencies working in the LTTE-controlled and newly cleared areas do not want to jeopardise their access to the populations they serve, and therefore rarely speak publicly about their observations. In addition to this, the international media find it difficult to report on a situation where the suffering is not easily seen and the country is of little strategic importance. A widely distributed report that enables participants to be heard is therefore central to increasing understanding about the situation.

For humanitarian aid workers

In the Wanni, most expatriate workers are on short-term 'emergency' contracts; a minority are on six-month to two-year contracts. Expatriate workers tend to be in positions of power in terms of decision-making and therefore need information from a wide range of sources on which to base these decisions. In this context, the LTD project can serve as a useful source of participants' views, rather than relying on the ubiquitous organisational voice. While every INGO and UN agency in northern Sri Lanka conducts needs assessments and evaluations, this information is generally kept within the agency or shared informally. LTD provides a public record of the opinions of the displaced.

National staff of humanitarian agencies are often assumed to have a detailed understanding of the situation in their communities, and most often they do. However, they rarely have an opportunity to reflect upon the situation in a comprehensive and structured way in order to unravel some of their everyday observations. LTD can provide a mechanism and tools to do this, thereby enriching the analysis. The aim of LTD is to assist humanitarian aid workers to design better programmes.

For the target community itself

'Who ever rules us, we are not bothered: we want peace' (man in Jaffna District, 1998)

'Our problem is not a shortage of cooking pots or shelter. Our problem is the war. If you offer cooking pots, we will take them; but if you ask what you can really do for us, we will say help to stop the fighting. If you can do anything to help bring peace, we will be able to take care of ourselves and stop being a burden to you' (woman in Kilinochchi District, 1997)

The civilian residents of the Wanni and Jaffna realise that they have only limited forums in which to make themselves heard, especially on sensitive topics such as peace. The opportunity to share thoughts and opinions with members of their own communities, particularly in the knowledge that these remarks will reach a wider audience, is important to participants. They want outsiders to know and understand how they feel about their situation.

'When we departed, the community waved us out and expressed interest in a future LTD process. They stressed the importance of us telling their story to important people in the uncleared and cleared areas of Sri Lanka and beyond Sri Lanka' (research facilitator, Kilinochchi District, 1998)

Helping residents in conflict-affected areas to be heard effectively is one step in the process of enabling them to claim their basic rights. The LTD project is used to uphold the rights of IDPs and other disaster-affected people to humanitarian assistance and protection. The witnessing role that INGOs play in upholding these rights is important, especially in Sri Lanka, where there is limited access to conflict-affected areas, where operational roles are restricted, and work through partners is so limited.

This particular methodology and process emerged in the context of Sri Lanka for a number of reasons. The displacement of people there has been protracted, and a large number have been displaced many times. The predicament of civilians is rarely allowed to reach 'disaster' levels, but teeters on the edge continually. Its status as an 'emergency' is therefore questionable. At the same time, access for humanitarian agencies is strictly limited (as discussed above). Anthropological information on the Sri Lankan Tamil culture, pre-war and during the war, is extremely scarce, and good information on preferences and habits is not available. Combined with Sri Lanka's non-strategic position and low international profile, this means that the needs of IDPs are less visible, and their voices almost silenced. LTD was designed with these limitations in mind, and attempts to meet these challenges. However, while it was designed specifically for these conditions, its concept and methodology are flexible and widely applicable.

Objectives of the research, 1996–1998

1996: Kilinochchi

- To record the process of displacement as it took place in Kilinochchi District and to determine its trends.
- To investigate relief — current priorities and delivery mechanisms.
- To explore gender-related dimensions of the displacement.

1997: Kilinochchi and Mullaitivu

- To gather first-hand information about the needs of the recent IDPs and especially public attitudes and intentions regarding the displaced and their (potential) return home.
- To assist the Oxfam relief programme to tailor packages of non-food relief items (NFRI) to fit the actual needs of the displaced.
- To give a broader and lasting voice to the displaced people.

1997: Mannar

- To evaluate the impact of recent relief interventions on the displaced adults and children, with a view to improving the effectiveness and relevance of such activities in the future.
- To identify the basic problems and prioritise the needs of displaced communities through participatory discussions with men, women, and children, and to identify potential long-term interventions that would complement short-term relief initiatives.

1998: the Wanni

- To identify and prioritise the needs of the displaced and host communities, and to identify potential long-term interventions that would complement short-term relief initiatives.
- To identify people's coping mechanisms and capacities in order to optimise future interventions.
- To give a broader and lasting voice to displaced people themselves.
- To practise and evaluate Oxfam and SCF's use of participatory assessment techniques.

1998: Jaffna

- To understand people's preparations, expectations and support systems on their return to Jaffna and to identify people's views on potential interventions.
- To improve understanding among the donor community about the coping strategies and views on assistance of families living in Jaffna.
- To lobby for programmes that will have a beneficial impact on people's lives.

In each year of the research, the objectives have been redefined in relation to the information needs of the programmes and the situation on the ground. In 1996, the LTD report concentrated on listening to the vulnerable groups that had been identified already. Listening was concentrated specifically on residents of welfare centres, those living with friends and relatives, and those living on the streets. It enabled those who had been displaced to express their views, and it assisted relief agencies to design more appropriate interventions, especially in relation to NFRI distributions and access to water. The report also provided first-hand information to donor and diplomatic bodies wishing to have a better understanding of the situation in the Wanni. It also highlighted aspects of programming that required more attention. Most importantly, it was the first written document after the 1995 mass displacement that reflected people's individual experiences.

In April 1997, Oxfam repeated and expanded the LTD exercise to listen to the displaced and host communities in all Assistant Government Agent (AGA) civil-service administration divisions in the LTTE-controlled areas of Kilinochchi and Mullaitivu Districts.

The 1997 LTD report examined the effectiveness of the relief interventions for those originally displaced from Jaffna and those newly displaced or redisplaced from Kilinochchi, which was captured by the SLA in November 1996. It also defined on-going issues for the communities in the Wanni, specifically looking at the relationships between the host and displaced communities. In this second year of the research, a more specific examination of the relationship between the host and displaced communities was chosen, because this had been identified as a topic needing more analysis. The research objectives incorporated this focus. SCF joined Oxfam in conducting this research and was also involved in deciding and refining the methodology that was employed.

In September 1997, SCF undertook similar research that considered issues relevant to displaced children and communities in the Mannar District, an LTTE-controlled area. This research, supported by Oxfam staff, concentrated specifically on the impact of relief interventions on children; it was used as a lobbying tool to encourage the provision of more appropriate child-focused relief items. The SCF report also looked more closely at the effect of large-scale displacement into the Mannar District resulting from the 1997 Edi Bala and Jaya Sikuru military operations.

The objectives of LTD in 1998 evolved out of the 1996 and 1997 research. This third phase was a collaborative effort by Oxfam and SCF. The objectives were defined through detailed discussions between the research facilitators and other colleagues, who strove to incorporate many of the ideas contained in the previous years' research. There were three main concerns. First, it was felt that participants should begin to set the discussion agenda. Secondly, there was a strong desire to increase understanding of displaced people's coping mechanisms. Lastly, there was a specific concern that the participatory work being undertaken with the research staff be made more explicit.

Similarly, the objectives of the Listening to the Returned (LTR) project in Jaffna were the result of the evolving situation there. After the mass exodus in 1995, many displaced people had returned to Jaffna. This was especially true in 1997 and 1998, when the conditions in the Wanni continued to deteriorate, and the situation on the peninsula was relatively stable. Families travelled through the slow but relatively safe government-approved route from Mannar Island to Trincomalee in the east and then by boat to Jaffna, or by the much riskier but more direct route, across the lagoon. Why they chose to return, what preparations families had to make, which route they chose to use and what experiences they faced needed to be documented, and an adaptation of the LTD project was seen as an appropriate mechanism to start this process.

'Before we were displaced we could find our village blindfolded, but we could not find it today even with our eyes open' (man in Jaffna District, 1998)

'Earlier, Puttur junction looked like a town; now it looks like a desert' (man in Jaffna District, 1998)

The objectives of the LTR project in Jaffna were broader, as this was the first such research to be conducted among the returnee/resettled population. Many respondents said this was the first time that anyone had talked with them about their situation. The principal objective of the research was to understand the process — from leaving the Wanni to resuming life in Jaffna. The research had the same objectives as the 1998 LTD project in the Wanni, but included additional objectives to provide insight into the specific situation on the peninsula.

'When we were in the Wanni, we believed our houses were still here, but when we returned we could not see that they had ever been there' (woman in Jaffna District, 1998)

Enabling the voices of the displaced to be heard is the key theme of the research. The pressure that agencies, donors, and government find themselves working under in an emergency situation normally makes this impossible. The objective of research carried out in an emergency context is to try to ensure that basic services are appropriate and that precious time and resources are not wasted. This type of project could therefore be useful in many different circumstances and could be used after natural as well as man-made disasters.

The objectives of such research need to be tailored to each situation. Completely separate objectives were drawn up for the Jaffna LTR research project to match the local circumstances. Initial discussions about the 1999 research included the possibility of expanding the research to the LTTE-controlled areas of eastern Sri Lanka, a place where people remain even more isolated than the residents of the Wanni. In all cases, gathering together the main stakeholders and working through a process of identifying the knowledge gaps would have to be the first step in the process.

Why listen to the displaced? — A summary

- Most emergency situations are characterised by top-down solutions that do not always take into account the opinion of the displaced/refugees.

- There is a great need for local information in emergency situations, but little recorded information readily available.

- Donors, government officials, and policy makers often do not have direct access to displaced/refugee populations and need information about their situation.

- Local NGOs in northern Sri Lanka are not always community-oriented and are therefore not necessarily a good source of objective, neutral information about the population.

- Other ethnic groups, the media, and interested parties have extremely limited access to the displaced population.

- Humanitarian aid workers often lack adequate information about the broader context of the crisis.

- The displaced community wants to be heard, but has few forums in which to speak.

3 How to listen to the displaced: methodology

Conventional and professionally respectable methods for rural research are often inefficient. The search is for approaches which are open to the unexpected, and able to see into, and out from, the predicament of the rural poor themselves. (Chambers 1983)

This chapter describes the methods used over the three years of the project and reviews the advantages and disadvantages of each year's methodology. It is written specifically for practitioners who might want to replicate the project and need a clear explanation of the actual methodology and an account of the kinds of results achieved by the various methods employed over the years.

The LTD methodology has changed slightly each year to reflect the changing information needs of the specific programme. As the project has progressed, there has been increasing emphasis on the involvement of the participants, in order that their voices are heard more clearly and their views represented more effectively. Indeed, in the first report of 1996, a general summary of what participants said, plus a few case studies, was the major focus of the report. The report was less inclusive because the situation was new and aid workers needed information to implement relief programmes. In the 1997 report, the introduction of a few quotes enabled participants' voices to be heard for the first time. By 1998, the methodology allowed the participants to set the agenda for discussion. While the focus of the LTD project has always been to enable 'voices' to be heard, there are many different research methodologies that allow this, so the project has tried to use methodologies that give participants the most chance to be heard. Outlined below are some of the strategies that have been employed.

LTD is more than just a 'one-off' piece of research. It is a process of action research from which results will be used to effect change. This change may be in the policies and practices of various institutions and organisations. It is a process that follows a cycle similar to a project development cycle, but with specific activities related to each turn of the wheel. See Figure 1.

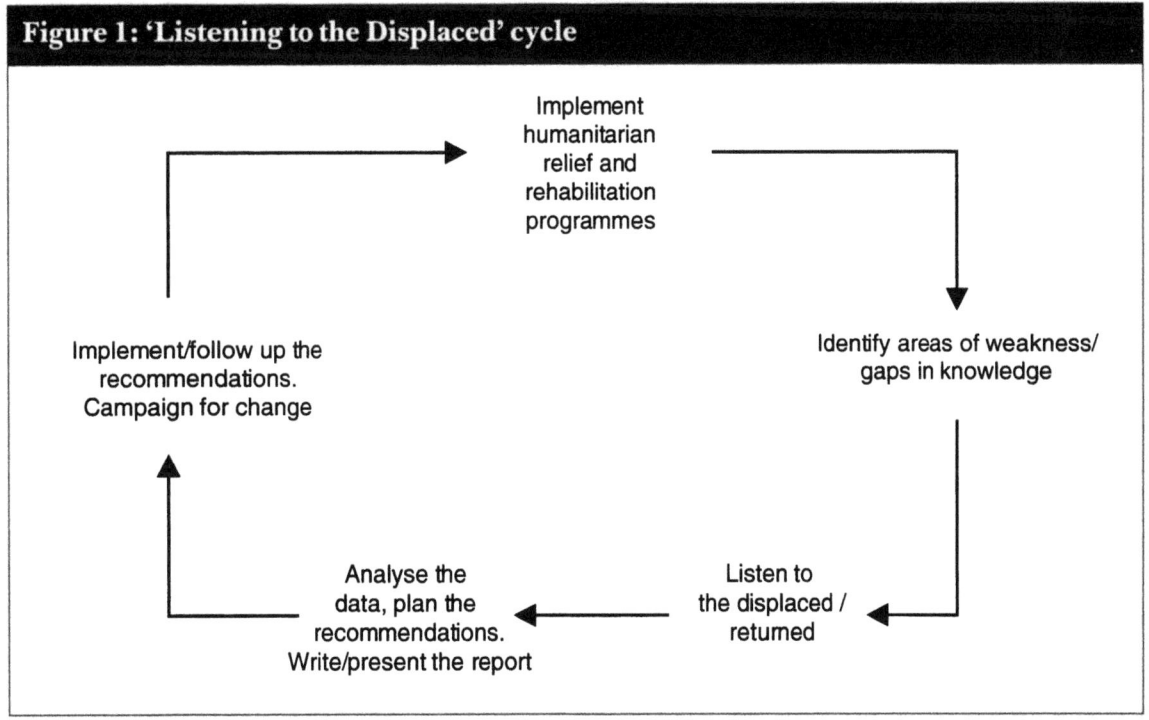

Figure 1: 'Listening to the Displaced' cycle

This project cycle is continuous, but also very slow. While it may appear straightforward and seem to be moving in one direction, in reality some parts of the cycle overlap. The project is always following up the recommendations of earlier reports, always defining weaknesses and gaps in knowledge, and always getting on with the day-to-day work of implementing humanitarian programmes.

How to listen: early days[5]

Semi-structured interviews

The original methodology employed by the LTD project in 1996 included a semi-structured interview technique.

Most questioning was guided by a checklist of themes to be covered. Group interviews, interviews with family groups, and some individual interviews were conducted. Structured exercises were used to determine people's preferences for non-food relief items. (Oxfam 1996)

The mixed methodology produced a great deal of diverse information, which provided a good general overview of the situation and the needs of the participants. This was exactly what was needed just months after the initial displacement. The exercises on NFRI also illustrated clearly that different participants accorded priority to different items, depending on their living situation. For example, street dwellers felt they needed a very different package of items from those living with friends and relatives. The outcomes of the research resulted in more appropriate targeting strategies being developed.

Focus groups

In the second year the Oxfam research employed a focus-group methodology.[6] According to the 1997 report:

In devising the list of topics to guide the focus groups, questions were reviewed so the primary focus would reflect areas within the Oxfam and SCF operational mandates. They were vetted so that the wording would convey minimum possible preconceptions to the respondents. They endeavoured to avoid 'leading' questions that would bias the people's spontaneous responses. When this process was completed in English it was repeated in Tamil, so that precise yet common terms were used, and respondents would be as free as possible to express their own needs and observations. (Oxfam 1997)

Table 2: Relief goods test results, 1996

People living on the street	People living with friends and relatives	People living in welfare centres
Mixed group Plastic sheeting Bed sheets Hurricane lamps Plastic buckets Mats Rice pot Clay pans Knife and scraper *Women's group* Kitchen utensils Shelter Big bucket Rice pot Water pot *Men's group* Shelter Curry pots Water pots Hurricane lantern Big bucket	*Mixed group* Plastic bucket Hurricane lantern Bed sheet Rice pot Plastic sheet	*Mixed group* Cooking pot and spoon Plastic sheeting Hurricane lantern Large bucket Clay cooking pans Cloth for menstruation Cloth (3 metres) Bed sheets Soap Mats

The idea was to design a list of questions for the focus groups that would cover general areas but could also be used in subsequent years in order to develop a longitudinal knowledge base about the situation (see Appendix 2 for a full list of the questions). This approach has merit in that it can provide a snapshot of the situation, using the same indicators over time. In addition, to cross-check data for gender-related and age-related sensitivities, the initial questions were asked in a general community group, but a separate meeting was then held with the women and children to explore in greater depth issues of specific concern to them.

Morgan (1993) suggests the following guidelines to decide when the use of focus groups is appropriate:

1 When there is a power differential between participants and decision makers.
2 Where there is a gap between professionals and their target audiences.
3 When investigating complex behaviours and motivations.
4 To learn more about the degree of consensus on a topic.
5 When there is a need for a friendly research method that is respectful and not condescending to the target audience.

These conditions are often present among refugees and displaced people. Whether or not focus groups are appropriate for a situation needs to be evaluated against the situation itself.

Focus groups can be an excellent source of information for researchers. One of the advantages of using this type of format is that it guides the gathering of information, ensuring that areas of interest for the research are covered in sufficient detail. Certainly, the checklist of key questions devised by the Oxfam and SCF teams in 1997 was quite a comprehensive survey of the situation. Focus groups, using the types of questions outlined in Appendix 2, are a particularly useful way of collecting a large cross-section of data for analysis and can be very inclusive in their scope.

In Year 2 of the work SCF joined the project, and in early 1997 some of their staff participated in the fieldwork. In addition, SCF went on to conduct a more focused research project entitled 'Listening to the Displaced in Mannar District', which was the geographic area where SCF programmes were focused. Oxfam staff participated in the fieldwork for the SCF report. This meant that the research objectives and methodology had to be decided jointly. It also

Table 3: Samples of focus-group questions, 1997

1 NFRI
• Did you receive any non-food relief items?
• If so, what were the items you received?
• How long were you displaced before receiving relief items?
• Did anyone come to you, before or after you were given the items, to discuss your needs?
• Were the items that you received useful and adequate?

2 Water
• What are your sources of water?
• How far away?
• Who collects water for your house?

3 Health and issues of gender, youth, and disability
• What is your access to health care? Distance and frequency of clinics, hospitals, mobile clinics?
• Is there any indigenous health care available locally?
• What are the most common diseases in your area?
• Are you aware of any counselling services available in this area?
• Are there disabled people in your location?
• Is anyone caring for unaccompanied children in your location?

4 Household incomes
a) For IDPs:
• What were your major income sources before displacement?
• What are your major sources of income now?
• What opportunities are there for women?
• Do the children work?
b) For hosts:
• How do you earn your living here?
• Have the economy/health/social relations been affected by the displacements?

5 NGOs
• What are the primary problems in this community?
• Are you aware of any organisations assisting with these problems?
• What kind of assistance have you received? When?
• Do you have any suggestions to improve the assistance?

meant that a common understanding had to be built up between the agencies. The 1997 SCF report made 'significant changes' to the earlier checklist of questions agreed between the agencies, in order to focus more specifically on children's issues. These questions were used to conduct focus groups in communities in Mannar District LTTE-controlled areas. After the focus-group results had been examined, it was decided to augment this information further with a series of PRA activities (Daily Routine Diagrams, Matrix Scoring, and Livelihood Analysis). These activities were used to gather more specific information about children's relief needs.

The most innovative aspect of the research in 1997 was its focus on both the voice of the displaced and that of the host community. Research on displaced and refugee populations too often neglects to examine the impact on the host community, and the vital area of interaction between the displaced and their hosts. The research in 1997 drew attention to the strain experienced by the host community in the Wanni and led to a number of programmes designed specifically to support them. The research also highlighted the tense relationship between the displaced and their hosts over access to resources such as water, land, schools, and health services. These findings were all considered in subsequent programme design.

How to listen: later days

The methodology used in 1996 and 1997 has been described to indicate ways of conducting such research, but greater detail will be given about the 1998 research, which grew from the experience of the first two years. The original methodologies of 1996 and 1997 were designed to elicit specific information about the humanitarian relief effort. In 1998, a methodology was employed that let participants set the discussion agenda and prioritise the issues that they wanted to discuss. Although a structure was provided, there was more freedom for the participants to describe issues and concerns. It was decided that enabling the participants to lead the discussion was an important part of effective listening. The methodology was also founded on the idea that 'People who begin to voice their personal or group experience can begin to understand it and act on it' (Slim and Thompson 1993). The research methodology also follows from the seminal work of Robert Chambers (1983) and Stan Burkey (1993), which encouraged development workers to listen to their counterparts.

As outlined in Figure 1, the LTD project follows a cyclical process. This process, examined in more depth and with extra steps added, is outlined in Figure 2. It will be described in more detail below.

The methodology for the 1998 LTD project was ratified at meetings between the key facilitators in Oxfam and SCF. The objectives, focus, and methods were discussed and agreed upon after reviewing the earlier research. Recognised information-gaps in the Wanni and Jaffna during this planning phase were taken into account, as well as the views of staff, former research participants, and colleagues. There was agreement that the methodology would attempt to draw out six key pieces of information:

1. Changes in the situation over the last year.
2. The communities' major problems, worries, and priorities.
3. Their current coping mechanisms for dealing with these problems.
4. The efficacy of outside interventions in responding to these problems.
5. People's capacities for solving their own problems.
6. The community's views on what outsiders (INGOs, LNGOs, government, churches, etc.) should do about the problems.

How to collect the information

A strategy was devised that would enable the participants to lead the conversations as much as possible and be involved to the fullest extent in thinking through issues and problems, rather than simply listing them. This method was thought to be worth piloting to see if it allowed greater inclusion of the participants' voice. A description of the actual steps in the research process follows.

The teams

In the Wanni, three teams, each comprising 4–5 Oxfam and SCF staff, were selected and trained. The staff of one LNGO and one UN agency also participated in the research and training. These teams worked with preselected communities in the field for four days—including a weekend, to ensure the participation of school children.

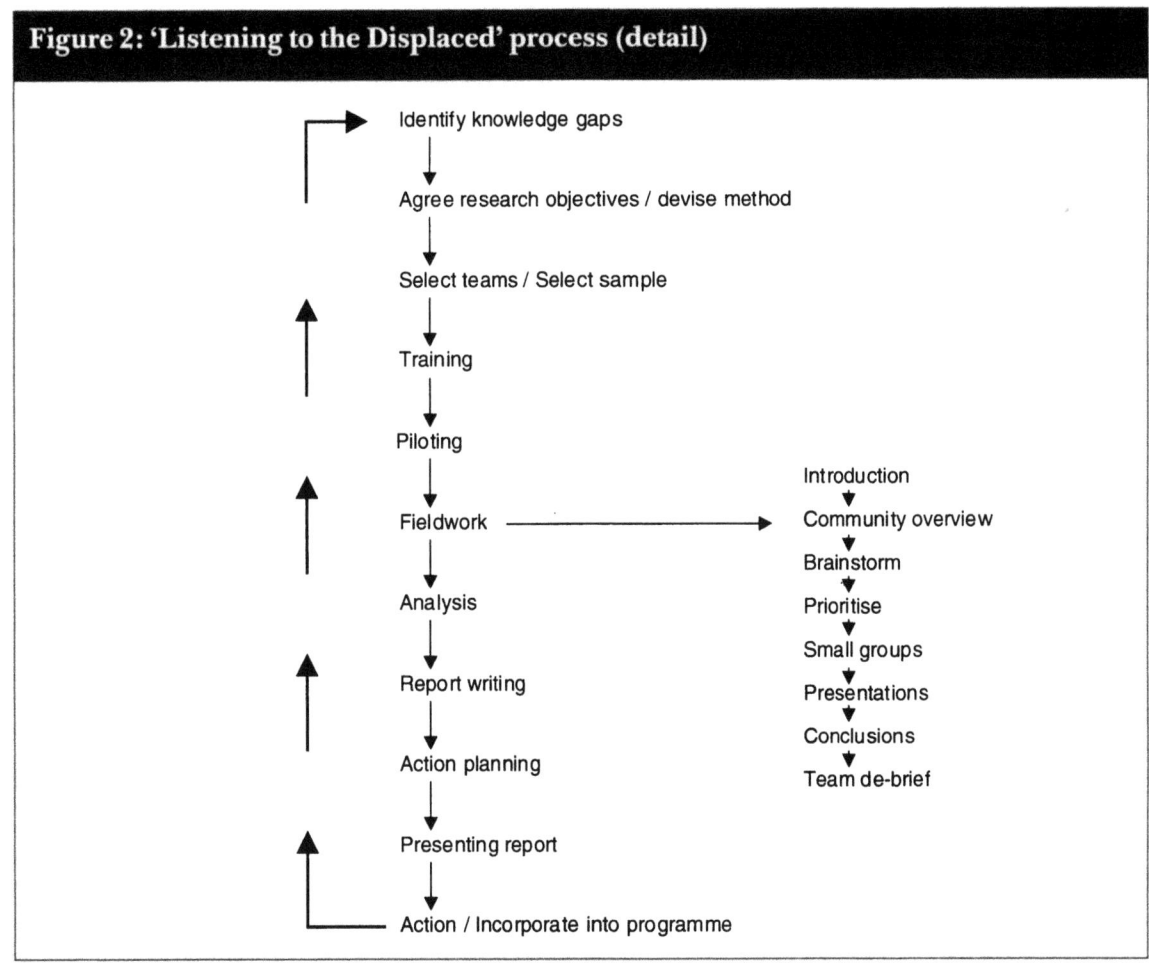

Figure 2: 'Listening to the Displaced' process (detail)

They met with two groups of participants per day. In Jaffna, two teams were selected and trained. They were predominantly SCF staff, plus two Oxfam staff and three participants from local community groups. These teams worked in the field for five days, meeting one group per day because of security constraints.[7]

Introduction

Upon arriving at a pre-selected site, the research team gathered a group for an introductory session which lasted about three hours — see the section below on 'Choosing the research participants' for details of how this was done. Groups ranged in size from 19 to 244 participants, but the average number of participants was approximately 100. When a group had been gathered, a general introduction was provided. This was a crucial part of the work, as most participants' experience with NGOs had been in the context of relief distributions or assessment for projects. The introduction needed to state clearly the project objectives: to hear what people had to say and enable their voices to be heard outside their region. Great care had to be taken not to raise participants' expectations that projects were being developed or assessed, but rather that the task was to listen and represent their voices to the best of the team's ability. It was also important to introduce each team-member and talk a little bit about his or her work. This provided a context into which the participants could fit the research teams, so that they knew they were talking to a range of aid workers, not government officials. The introduction also tried to make it clear that participants were free *not* to contribute. This was probably a novel idea to people who would not usually have had a choice about attendance at community meetings. However, few chose to leave.

The participant groups in the Wanni were typically 35 per cent women, 23 per cent men, and 42 per cent children. Sessions were scheduled around lunch, which is the main meal of the day — one session before and one session after. In Jaffna the groups were typically 46 per cent women, 24 per cent men, and 30 per cent children, and most sessions were held before lunch each day.

Community overview

Once the objectives of the meeting were clear, a general discussion was initiated about the settlement and the services available within it. During this part of the conversation, rough estimates of the population and an idea of the available services were discussed — water, health, education, and others. Participants were then asked to comment on the general situation over the past year.

'The army hassles us more because we are poor, and the big people walk about freely' (man in Jaffna District, 1998)

This discussion served as an icebreaker for the participants. It also gave the teams a chance to identify the real talkers among the participants and to observe how the group dynamics worked. This introductory discussion often provided a fairly clear idea of how the participants would characterise their community and the changes in it over the past year. This was surprising, in that it was an unfocused general discussion not intended for serious data collection. However, it often provided key information that could be examined in more detail during the sessions described below.

During this section of the LTR research in Jaffna, participants were asked about their return to Jaffna, the preparations they had made, their expectations, and the route they used. While this provided a general overview, it might, on reflection, have been more useful to examine this question in a more structured way, because the information gathered was sometimes sketchy.[8] What it clearly indicated was that this area required further research.

Brainstorming exercise

Once the topics in the general discussion were exhausted, the participants were asked to describe their main worries and problems. A volunteer from among the participants wrote these issues on a flipchart.[9] A special effort was made to ensure that all present — women, men, and children — took part in this process, even if their particular concerns had already been listed. Individuals who had not spoken were asked for their opinions. Encouraging participants who were quiet in the initial overview discussion and brainstorming activities, and soliciting their direct input, illustrated to the group and these individuals that their ideas were valued. This was especially true for children, the disabled, and widows, who became more involved as a result.

The focus in 1998 was on the analysis of major problems or worries, as defined by the participants. The methodology is flexible, however, and it would also be possible to set an agenda of issues for discussion if time was limited or researchers had specific information needs. While outsiders set the structure in which discussion took place, the emphasis was on learning from the communities, in order to make aid programmes more responsive and appropriate.

Group prioritisation

When the general list was complete, it was held up for all the participants to see. It was read through, and final additions were made. The group was then asked to pinpoint the biggest problem from the list. When that had been agreed, the second largest problem was identified, and so on until at least the top five problems had been prioritised; in some cases this was extended up to ten priorities. Consensus on this was generally reached quite quickly and was fairly uniform. Care must be taken that all voices are heard during this phase, not only the loudest ones. While this 'verbal consensus' method worked quite well with the Tamil groups, different methods might be employed in cases where consensus cannot be reached this easily. They might include individual ranking exercises, or asking participants to vote — verbally or with beans, stones, or other materials. If working in a cultural context where women's voices are often not heard in group work, it may be more advantageous to form sex-segregated groups for the ranking and see if the outcomes are similar or different. This was not a particular issue for the Tamil groups, as women were active participants in the discussions.

'The mines are everywhere. Only when our husbands and children return at the end of the day do we know whether they still have their legs' (woman in Jaffna District, 1998)

Eliud Ngunjiri (1998) criticises the listing/prioritisation of 'problems' as a starting point in PRA work or research. He sees this as unnecessarily disempowering and negative.

Starting a discussion in this way highlights how problem-ridden a community is. Instead, he recommends starting with an examination of the resources and capacities in a community and then looking for gaps. This process of 'positive self-discovery' is a more optimistic way of discussing community issues. While LTD comes around to this in its discussion of capacities and coping mechanisms, starting in a positive way could be a useful adaptation of the LTD research methodology.

Small-group work

When there was a mutually agreed priority list, the participants were split into small groups by sex and age — a women's group, a men's group, and a children's group. Each small group was asked to look at two problems in detail: the major problem from the community priority list, plus the problem that seemed the most important to them as a group. This was to ensure the collection of detailed information about the most important problem in each community, taking gender and age into consideration, and also to find out what the next most pressing problem was for each individual group.

Information was gathered on these two problems by asking each group to answer four key questions:

- What is the community doing about the problem now?
- What have others done about this problem?
- What could they (members of the group) do about the problem in the future?
- What could others do about this problem?

Table 4: Key questions reviewed in 1998

What is the community doing about the problem now?

The information sought here is how people, households, and communities are currently coping with this problem. Are they actively doing something about it? What are they doing? Who is doing it? And what is the impact (social, economic, cultural) of their actions?

Key questions
- At a personal level: what are people doing themselves about the problem?
- At a household level: what are people in a family doing? Who is doing it?
- At a community level: what are community members doing? Who in the community is doing it?

What have others done about the problem?

This seeks to discover the results of past interventions. Were they successful or not, and why? Who did them? How could interventions be improved?

Key questions
- Who has done something about the problem — government authorities, non-government authorities, politicians, churches, individuals?
- What did they do?
- What was the impact? Was it useful or not useful?
- Did it/does it work? Is it successful?
- What could have been done better?

What could the community do about the problem in the future?

This set of questions seeks to identify what capacities, what strengths, what possibilities the community members see for tackling the problem themselves, so that future NGO interventions might act to strengthen these rather than replace them.

Key questions
- At a personal level: what could people themselves do about the problem?
- At a household level: what could people in a family do? Who should do it?
- At a community level: what could community members do? Who in the community should do it?

What could others do about this problem?

These questions try to find out what, in the community's view, others could/should do about the problem, so that future interventions might be most practical for the people.

Key questions
- Who should do something about the problem — government authorities, non-government authorities, politicians, churches, individuals?
- What should they do?
- What would the impact be?

What the small-group work did was to elicit information about coping mechanisms (what they are currently doing about the problem), about capacities (what they could do about the problem), information about the efficacy of past interventions (what others have done about the problem),[10] and suggestions from the community about what future interventions would be useful (what others could do about this problem). Before the actual discussion of the problem started, there was a brief discussion about what the group felt the essence of the problem or worry was, in order to ensure that they were all talking about the same thing.

When the small group was discussing its coping mechanisms and capacities, each response was recorded as an individual, household, or community action. Questions about what participants were doing at each level were also asked, in order to develop a clearer understanding of the participants' experiences and strengths.

When examining past and future interventions, there was a focus on 'impact', both what had happened and what was perceived as still necessary. In the case of past interventions, the participants also had to evaluate what had happened and their role in it. For example, in one community in Kilinochchi District in 1998, there was reflection on the results of an LNGO seed-distribution programme carried out to ease unemployment problems. While participants felt this was a useful intervention, it had not had the intended impact, because (the participants felt) the LNGO staff implemented their 'own ideas' rather than those of the residents. The LNGO gave groundnut seed to people who had paddy land. At the same time, the participants reflected that they had not been assertive enough in making their feelings known, because they feared it might jeopardise their chances of future assistance.

Information was recorded by a volunteer from each small group on a piece of flipchart paper broken into a grid. A sample of this grid is reproduced in Figure 3. It is similar to the grid for recording the information included in Appendix 3.

Figure 3: Recording the information

Problem: UNEMPLOYMENT   **Type of group:** WOMEN

What are you doing about the problem?	What could you do about the problem?
Personal: Agricultural labouring Poultry farming Stitching work Goat / cattle farming *Household:* Home gardens Small business Farming – rainy season *Community:* Nothing!	*Personal:* Expand poultry farming Stitching training *Household:* Expand home gardens More farming *Community:* Talk to NGO about credit. Make a women's cooperative to sell baskets

What have others done about the problem?	What could others do about the problem?
1 NGO gave 1/2 acre of land and seeds for cultivation But never gave hoes or fertiliser Didn't know how to grow 2 Government gave work rebuilding roads Need this more regularly A Need regular work / income B Need support from NGO's to learn	✓ Provide access to money/credit to do farming/small business ✓ Provide access to irrigated land ✓ Access to agricultural inputs, sprayers, water pumps, fertilisers NGO's + helping organisations should do this!

Presentations

When all small groups had completed their exploration of the problems, the plenary reconvened. Representatives from each group were invited to come and present their findings. This was followed by a discussion and comparison of each group's points and information. This was especially valuable in the case of major problems that all three groups had worked on. Where children had been asked to make drawings, they were requested to show them to the group and explain their work.

Conclusion

In the conclusion, the research team summarised the work that had been completed and asked the participants about the next steps. Did they want to receive a copy of the report? Were they going to take action themselves about their problems? What did they think of the exercise?

'So many people are coming, asking and then going. Please don't do that' (man in Mullaitivu District, 1998)

While some of the participants perceived the research team as no different from the myriad assessment teams that came through their villages, many participants thanked the LTD research team for really listening to them and spending time discussing their problems and worries. Some participants said that they felt better for having done so. Appreciation for being 'listened to' has been expressed in all years of the work. Residents of the Wanni and Jaffna are not only interested in the projects, but often appreciate the opportunity to discuss and reflect on problems and worries in a structured way. Participants noted that the research format used in 1998 also allowed them to think through what they could do about the problem and left them with community-based ideas of how to move forward.

Team debrief

As soon as possible after the conclusion of the community meeting, the research team held a 'debriefing' session to record all the information. This was essential to ensure completeness and accuracy while events remained fresh in the team's minds. The flipcharts created by the volunteer scribes provided the guide for transferring information on to a site summary form (see Appendix 3).[11] There was also discussion to identify the other perceptions that had been expressed, and the teams recorded observations that they had made in the communities. At this point, the information was translated back into English and recorded in English; this would not be necessary if the report was to be in the original language only. In Sri Lanka, the use of English facilitated the report writing and communication across ethnic groups.

'We will stay together as a family. If a shell comes, we will all die together. I don't want my children to be orphans' (young woman, Kilinochchi District, 1998)

During the fieldwork, team members were asked to remember specific things that participants had said which were particularly representative of the overall situation or were especially poignant. These 'quotes' were recorded during the team debrief and later served to illustrate points more clearly in the reports and to allow the participants' own words 'to be heard'.

A key aspect of the feedback session, besides recording the information for the report, was to reflect on the session itself in terms of participation, group facilitation, community–team interaction, and body language (see Training section below). Feedback on the research team's performance was also discussed.

The full participatory sessions generally lasted about three hours, from the time the team arrived until the main group dispersed after the conclusion. Sessions with fewer participants could sometimes be concluded more quickly, although some lasted longer because discussion of a particular issue was unresolved or particularly interesting, or because strategies to keep it interesting were being employed. In 1998, in one village in Mullaitivu District, for example, the children's group was very large, so the researcher leading the group interspersed questions with games and songs. This helped to keep the children's attention and ensured answers of good quality.

Which method to choose?

Each year's methodology has its merits: interviews used in 1996, focus groups in 1997, and the more open-ended technique used in 1998. Where there is a lack of information about a situation, such as in a new emergency or displacement, it may be more appropriate to use the interview or focus-group methodology, because the information needs that are apparent at the beginning of any emergency can be met more quickly.

LTD-type techniques are not completely new in Sri Lanka. S.P.F. Seneratne (a social anthropologist) used listening and observation techniques to gather information to bridge the gaps between the ideas of government planners and villagers (Seneratne 1978 in Chambers 1983). Investigating the techniques that have previously worked well in a country, before embarking on this type of project, is a useful investment for the selection of appropriate research methods for particular circumstances. Whatever methodology is selected, it will need to be adapted to the field conditions at the research site.

Where an emergency situation is more settled and there is some understanding of the structures of assistance and patterns of displacement, a methodology that allows the communities to set the tone and topics of the discussions might be more appropriate. The choice of methodology may also be influenced by the need to enable the voices of the displaced to be heard in the report. There are other research methods, such as participant-observation, oral history, or surveys, which the LTD project has not tried to use. These methodologies might be deemed appropriate for other situations. The LTD methodology would be unsuitable where quantitative data are needed.

How to listen to the displaced: a summary

- Decide which methodology is most appropriate for the specific information needs of your project and adapt the methodology accordingly.

- Define the research questions that need to be answered:
  - If they are quantitative, consider using a survey.
  - If they are qualitative but YOU need to gather specific information about the displaced, consider using semi-structured interviews or focus groups.
  - If they are qualitative and aim to increase understanding of coping mechanisms and people's capacities, as well as the effectiveness of past and future interventions, consider using the participatory activities described here.

4 Things to consider when researching displacement

In conducting any type of research with human subjects, there will be a number of issues that need to be addressed. Researchers in the fields of anthropology, geography, history, and sociology have examined these issues in detail in relation to their own work. Some of the considerations that were important in the Sri Lankan context are outlined here as a starting point.

Training

The moderator is the instrument in a focus group interview. If the moderator as the data collection instrument is not prepared, not attentive or not skilful, then the results will be just as bad as in a poorly prepared survey questionnaire. (Morgan 1993)

One key objective of the research was to practise and develop staff members' skills in PRA techniques and generally promote field skills. This was especially important in the context of Sri Lanka, where many NGO workers join agencies with no prior community-based experience. It is often assumed that they are aware how their physical position in social situations or meetings, their body language, verbal language, facilitation skills, and general consideration for others affect their communications and relationships with people. The reality is that agency staff often have no such experience or understanding at all. Simple exposure to these ideas, practice, and immediate feedback on their use in fieldwork can produce positive results very quickly. The abilities and attitudes of the research teams are crucial to the success of the research.

Before beginning fieldwork, the facilitators conducted one and a half days' training on facilitation skills and the LTD research methodology. This covered the basics of information collection (as outlined in the previous chapter), and also issues of facilitation in research.[12] Table 5 lists a number of specific issues of interest to the facilitators.

Table 5: Facilitation: key issues

Context

Position
- How was the spot selected for the group? Was it a good one?
- Where did you sit/stand? What impact did this have?
- Where did the participants sit/stand?
- Could you see/hear everyone? Could they see/hear you?

General observation
- The living context of the community
- The interaction between the community and researchers
- The interaction within the community

Facilitation

Listening
- Body language
- Stimulation of the group but control of their direction
- Analysing comments while listening and asking further questions
- Use of open and closed questions.

Focus
- Who are you looking at? Who are you focusing on? Who are you listening to? Everyone, or just certain members of the community?

Observation
- Who participates and who doesn't?
- Dominant versus 'invisible'/quiet people
- Sex and age of participants
- Interaction between the team and the community, and between community members themselves.

Status
- High versus low status and power roles
- Physical and personal status in the context of all the questions

Children
- Be aware that they know a lot!
- Pitch language at their level
- Ask easy questions
- Build up trust
- Provide stimulation and fun
- Ensure clarity
- Establish rules
- Use drawing

The first issue was positioning and observation. It is customary when visitors arrive in a Tamil village for someone to find them a chair — often taking school-children's chairs or teachers' chairs, even if school is in session. The session on positioning suggested that equality between the participants and the facilitators needed to be maintained. If there were not enough chairs or mats for everyone (a rarity unless the session was conducted in a school), everyone should sit on the ground. Participants like to get behind the facilitator, to avoid having to comment. Ensuring that this does not happen is important, and involved another simple technique that was reviewed and practised.

Observation skills were also discussed and practised in the training, and followed up with staff in the field. While observation skills were not relied on heavily for this particular research, their use as a data-collection tool was discussed. Issues about participants' relationships with one another and with the field workers were of specific interest in the context of observation.

Training researchers in listening skills focused on body language, the use of open and closed questions, and maintenance of group interest. It also involved giving guidance on how to listen while questioning, and using the revealed information to ask further questions. The body language, facial expression, and engagement levels of both researchers and participant groups were discussed and demonstrated. In subsequent fieldwork, use of good body language was identified, to reinforce good practice. During team debriefs, there was also discussion of the participants' reactions to the researchers, as observed via the participants' body language.

A major part of maintaining group interest revolved around keeping the conversation going, but ensuring that relevant information was being recorded as well. The research teams noticed that lulls in the conversation while information was being recorded often caused participants to lose focus. The researchers had to develop skills to keep participants talking, while ensuring that earlier points were recorded simultaneously. This was practised during the team-debriefing sessions. Role-play, in which one team member led the questioning and the others responded, was modelled on an actual situation encountered during the small-group work. Team members observed how the questions were asked (open or closed), to whom they were directed, and their impact (measured in terms of whether or not the groups kept talking). Team members and the facilitator made suggestions for improvement. Thinking critically after each session about potential improvements was an important way for members to learn about group facilitation.

At the same time, it is important for research facilitators to keep participant groups moving in one direction and stop them drifting too far from the task at hand. During the training session, one role-play illustrated participants wandering from or changing the topic, and played out how the facilitator would deal with this. The teams found that the most effective strategy was to recognise publicly the importance of what the speaker had said, but ask the group to return to that subject later and meanwhile focus on the issue at hand. This allowed the speaker to feel that he or she had been heard, but allowed the group work to progress.

During the training and after the field work, there were long discussions about questioning methods. There is a fine balance between 'leading' a discussion with questions and letting the questions and responses lead the discussion. Researchers need to consider whether responses are being questioned or simply accepted. For example, if participants say that unemployment is a problem in their community, research teams should be encouraged to find out as much about employment as possible, and how this relates to other issues such as shelter or education. Are the issues related? If so, how?

When a discussion was proceeding slowly and participants were not offering much information, the researchers found it helpful to ask a series of 'closed' questions such as: 'Do you work?', 'Do you earn income?', 'Does your family need additional income?'. *Yes* or *no* responses were followed with 'open' questions, such as: 'What do you do?', 'How do you earn income?', 'Why does your family need additional income?'. In this way hesitant or quiet participants were encouraged to speak.

During the training, questioning sessions were acted out as role-plays, and other researchers gave opinions on the thoroughness of the questioning and suggested additional questions that the role players might have asked to elicit more information. The learning point was the importance of questioning until a matter had been exhausted and all participants in a group had contributed their opinion. In the team debrief, the playing-out of questioning in a session was examined, and good practice was reinforced.

To reinforce observational skills, field workers were asked to observe the group participants, their age and sex, and to note any issues of concern. At the same time, they were asked to observe carefully who was participating and who was not, in order to ensure the inclusion of as many voices as possible.

'The major population group lacking in most groups was teenagers, who were often at school or in extra lessons. A better effort to target them should be made next year' (Wanni research group comments, 1998)

Status is another very important issue. Robert Chambers (1993) notes:

Staff working in rural areas distance themselves from rural people, showing their separate style and standing through clothing, shoes, vehicle, office, briefcase, documents and manner of speech.

This is certainly true in Sri Lanka and many other countries, and its manifestations were discussed during the training and the field work. One typical piece of behaviour is for field staff to carry a notebook and pen with them to the field. In the training, through group discussion, it was decided that the process of continually noting what people say actually detracts from the process of listening to them. Also such 'instruments of the trade' identify field staff as different from, and therefore potentially more important than, members of the community. The implications of this for researcher/community relations were discussed. It was agreed that field staff would not carry notebooks with them or make separate notes during the meetings, but could do so immediately afterwards if they felt it was necessary to help them remember key points. This practice is also being encouraged in the field.

Similarly, for Jaffna, there was discussion about whether the clothing worn by staff in the field had an impact on the way participants addressed them or what they told them. The wearing of saris (formal) versus skirts and blouses (casual) for women, of closed-toe shoes (formal) versus sandals (casual) for men, and the wearing of jewellery — an indication of wealth — by both sexes was debated without resolution. It was agreed that showing respect to the community being visited by dressing decently was important. There was also agreement that being conscious of one's visible wealth and status, especially in a class-conscious and caste-conscious society, was very important.[13]

The principles of all these topics were reviewed through group discussions and role-play. However, the best environment for training proved to be the field, and learning from these experiences took place during the team debriefs after each session.

During training, logistics were also reviewed. Reviewing and agreeing arrangements in advance is very important because of security concerns (aerial bombing and artillery shelling of military targets adjacent to roads or civilian areas) limited transportation resources (vehicles and fuel), radio-only communications, and limitations on time in the field. Team leaders, responsible for travel, food, accommodation, as well as collection and recording of information, were appointed. Initially, it had been hoped that daily radio contact between the three teams could be organised to facilitate uniformity of data collection and to sort out logistical problems. However, due to the timing of the sessions, travel constraints, and unreliable radio frequencies, this was not always possible. In Jaffna, this was less of an issue, because the two groups were working in close proximity to each other and could consult one another more easily. However, here there were other logistical constraints in the shape of security concerns — landmines and sensitive security checkpoints — and a shortage of vehicles.

Working with children

'I had a difficult child in my group. He wanted all of the attention. So I made him the leader of a younger children's group and asked him to supervise their work. This worked very well and he did a good job' (debrief notes, Mullaitivu District, 1998)

There were sometimes more than 100 children participating in any one session, and thus the children's groups presented special problems. A number of different strategies were used.[14] If there were large groups of children, one approach was to take selected children through the same exercise that the adults were completing. The rest would be asked to draw a picture on a specific topic. Following the 1997 SCF research, children were sometimes asked to draw their homes before and after displacement, and to discuss the differences.

Alternatively, they might be asked to draw a picture of the community's main problem — employment, food or shelter — and then discuss the drawing.

Interestingly, drawing pictures often proved very useful, even when it was relatively unsupervised. In one instance, a girl aged twelve led a group of younger children in composing an illustrated memo to the only aid agency they knew, to tell them about their situation. The formal small-group discussion was also sometimes interspersed with games or songs, to keep children interested and attentive.

'Our parents are willing to do any kind of labour job, but the people who live here say they don't have the skills to do them' (children in Kilinochchi District, 1998)

In all cases, in the concluding section of the meeting, the children were asked to explain to the adults what they had done. Whether children were presenting pictures that they had drawn, or were explaining what they thought their own coping mechanisms and capacities were, the looks of pride and of surprise on the adult participants' faces were an important part of recognising the value of children's input on larger problems. In as much as it illustrated to Oxfam staff the importance of children's voices in solving community problems, it also brought this message home strongly to the communities.

'I had to leave school to look after my brothers and sisters' (13-year-old girl with five siblings and no mother, in Kilinochchi District, 1998)

In the 1998 research, working with children and making them a focus of the work also illustrated that there were few adolescents at the sessions. This was seen as a worrying trend. It was recognised that this group needed to be targeted specifically in the next round of research.

Gender and women's voices

There is frequently a misperception that Tamil women are voiceless. Although in public life women still play a less visible role than men, their role is said to have become much less circumscribed than in the past. The most frequently cited example of this is: 'Before the war, women did not ride bicycles; now everyone rides.' While there is evidence that women did indeed ride bicycles before the war, the number of women riding them has increased dramatically. Shopping, which was a predominantly male activity in Tamil society before the war, is now visibly a more gender-equal task. The extent to which this is the result of widowhood and absent males, or is simply a choice on the part of women and men, is unknown. Women are also more visible in small-scale farming outside their homes, rather than being exclusively occupied with the indoor activities of food-preparation and child-rearing. This change is reflected in participants' comments, especially those made by children.

'Before we were displaced, our mothers didn't have to work, but now everyone goes for work' (child in Kilinochchi District, 1998)

Women have become much more involved in the public sphere since the conflict began. The image of LTTE female cadres doing everything that their male colleagues do — wearing trousers and in some cases cutting their hair short, driving trucks and motorbikes, going to the front line, handling weapons, and acting in positions of authority — must have had a profound effect on people's perceptions of women's capabilities. Even so, women still do not actually have the kind of equality that might be suggested by the fact that women comprise almost 40 per cent of the LTTE fighting force.[15]

Although Tamil women's voice is strong, it was important to observe which women were speaking in any particular context. In Tamil culture, where the status of single women and widows is different (and lower) than that of married women, it was important to ensure that all women's voices were heard, not just those who are more empowered by their culture to speak. Research teams were asked specifically to direct questions to women if they were not actively participating, and to ensure that all were taking part. Directly requesting participation of particular individuals (as discussed above) had a positive effect on encouraging their participation throughout the sessions.

Actually during the small-group work in 1998, the research teams noted that it was more difficult to facilitate the men's groups than the women's. The men were more reticent to speak. The reasons for this remain unclear. More consideration and investigation is needed before this research is repeated. It may signal the need for a different approach to encourage men's participation.

Listening to the disabled

'All members of the community participated. An example of this was a family where all the members were deaf. They participated actively in the discussions and were listened to' (research facilitator, Kilinochchi District, 1998)

Disabled people participated actively in the LTD project in 1998. This was more by providence than design, however. Disabled people encountered when participants were being gathered were specifically requested to attend. In the Wanni, though, the on-site gathering of participants may very well have inadvertently excluded many disabled people who needed more preparation time in order to participate. In Jaffna, on the other hand, where participation was pre-arranged, disabled people did participate, but their numbers were not visibly greater than in the Wanni. This is an issue that needs to be more carefully considered in the future.

Choosing the research participants

Assessment fatigue

'Always you NGOs are coming and asking information, but never doing anything' (widow in Kilinochchi District, 1998)

The phenomenon of 'assessment fatigue' was identified by Jok M Jok (1996) when selecting participants for research. In 1997, the Oxfam report states:

Nevertheless in ... a host community, no one made themselves available to be interviewed even though we had contacted them immediately prior to the planned meeting. The Grama Sevaka [head person of several villages] of the area explained that people were 'Tired of too many meetings with the movement and everyone else'.

Assessment fatigue is the result of people answering the continual, and often inappropriate, questions of assessment missions, without experiencing any subsequent results. To counter this problem, the LTD team made it very explicit during the introduction that their purpose was to listen and represent people's voices to others, and that the research was not an assessment mission. Nevertheless, participants complained of fatigue more than once during our discussions with them.

The best way to avoid this problem is for every assessment mission to act on its findings and to report back to each community. Assessment fatigue signals either that communication of the mission's results to the community is weak, or that nothing is actually resulting from many such missions. The message from the people is clear: use the information that we have given you, and avoid the temptation to start from scratch every time.

Consent

In all three years of the research, anonymity has been maintained, and names have never been recorded. Even references to villages are removed from the reports. Participants are free to withdraw if they wish. In some cases it is obvious that they do not want to participate. Consent to proceed should be agreed with the participants at the introductory stage of the research process. It was recognised that identifying individuals would not encourage people to speak. Daring to speak out about a situation is dangerous under authoritarian regimes. LTD in no way sets out to promote a political dialogue, but displacement, aid, and conflict are very political subjects.

However, there is also the issue of consent from the governing bodies. The Wanni is controlled by the LTTE. In Jaffna, the control is in the hands of the Sri Lankan government. Should these parties give consent for the research process? If they give consent but want to ensure 'positive results', they could influence the research data by restricting access to certain communities or by telling villagers what messages they should be giving. If they are not consulted, they can deny the credibility of any of the results of the research and refuse to countenance any of the lobbying efforts to change things.

Gaining the consent of the authorities, whoever they may be, is important in all contexts but can be a contentious issue in conflict-affected areas. In a situation like that in Sri Lanka, where one of the primary reasons for doing the research is because the voices of the displaced are not being heard, the controlling forces may feel threatened if attempts are made to encourage people to speak out. Generally speaking, it is essential to gain consent and acceptance for this type of research from the greatest possible number of stakeholders in the process. In 1998, the LTTE made it very clear that they wanted agencies to stop conducting research and actually implement programmes that met the 'obvious' needs of the people. Unfortunately, their own ideas of 'obvious' needs have not always accorded with displaced people's specific priorities. The question then becomes whether the voice of the participants or the acceptance of the authorities is more important. This needs to be evaluated in every cultural context.

Sampling methods

In the Wanni it seems that a 'random arrival' method of selecting participants works best, precisely because organised meetings at which attendance is not an option are the norm. This is not always possible, however, and care needs to be taken in considering the method of selection that is right for any given community. More formal sampling methods, such as random or cluster sampling, have not been employed for any of the LTD research. As LTD is not trying to be representative, but rather to illustrate trends, this has not been a problem thus far. Ensuring the participation of all groups is essential, however. In 1998, it was recognised that disabled people and adolescents were under-represented. This needs to be considered in the sampling-selection method used in future.

When selecting communities for study, there was an attempt to return to some of the communities surveyed in the previous year, and a cross-section of the communities visited by Oxfam and SCF was selected. They were not all included, because it was thought more important to try to cover a geographically representative area. This area — three sites in each of the nine AGA divisions in the LTTE-controlled areas of Kilinochchi, Mullaitivu, and Mannar Districts — was not necessarily representative of the population concentrations in the Wanni.[16] In Jaffna, as this was a new project, communities that were accessible within the research timeframe were selected.

It has never been an expectation of this research work that the same families would be tracked over time. Due to recurrent displacements, people may not be in the same location one year later or even six months later. There is a high degree of mobility in the Wanni. Indeed in 1998, when many of the 1997 sites were re-visited, large numbers of participants had moved on and an equal number of new people had moved in, occupying the homes of those who had left. While in some situations returning to actual families and tracing their experience over time would have merit as a longitudinal study, in the context of the Wanni, the best that a 'listening' exercise can offer is a longitudinal study of locations over time.

Bias

In 1998, the research project tried two methods of soliciting participants for the research. In the Wanni, the groups were chosen by simply asking members of the community if they had time to participate. This was done at the team's first meeting with the community upon arrival at the location. This method generally worked well, as there was a natural curiosity on the part of members of the community, and participants were especially pleased that there were separate activities for children.[17] While this method of choosing could have distorted the research results, because of participants' relative proximity to roads, to give balance researchers made a point of also seeking out more remote communities.

In Jaffna, due to security concerns and the sensitivity of the local military to spontaneous gatherings of large groups of people, all meetings had to be arranged in advance through the *Grama Sevakas* (GSs), who also informed the local military commanders of the project. This met with good results in most cases, but also led to some failures of communication and disappointment. Some communities may have thought that a distribution was planned, because most GSs have primarily encountered aid-agency representatives in the context of distribution or assessment for development projects. Indeed in many communities, the mere arrival of a white vehicle driven by an expatriate was enough to send people scurrying for their ration cards. Also, in at least one instance, the GS misunderstood the request and invited only adults to the gathering, assuming that all of the children had gone to school. As the meeting was held outside the actual community for security reasons — the community was close to an LTTE-controlled area and there were frequent exchanges between SLA and LTTE troops — there was no way to verify this. This did not meet with our experience in every other settlement, where school children were available for consultation, even at times when school was in session.

There was discussion among team members regarding the method of selection and the days of the week on which participants were surveyed, and whether this could have an impact on answers. There was some concern that those surveyed on weekdays were people with no regular work, or were school leavers, segments of the society with a potentially different viewpoint from the society as a whole. In the Wanni, the research was specifically scheduled to bridge the weekend in an attempt to include school children. In the Wanni also, unemployment was identified as the biggest concern, but the answers from sessions conducted on traditional working days did not differ from those conducted over the weekend. In Jaffna, where the research was conducted on weekdays only, this was an issue for concern.

The LTD research methodology has become more rigorous with each passing year, in attempting to gather information that will be valid in its conclusions. It draws upon the ideas and experiences of a number of researchers and practitioners.[18] It also attempts to be as unbiased as possible and to recognise its weaknesses. The issue of rigour in the research is one that needs more attention, but at the same time this should not overtake the first priority of listening to and representing the voices of the displaced.

Selecting the research teams

One of the very positive aspects of this work each year has been the direct involvement of the field staff in the project. In all years, the researchers have been Oxfam programme and administrative staff. When SCF joined the project in 1997, they also used their programme staff, in preference to contracting outside researchers to conduct the study. There have been several positive benefits, among them the following:

- Field staff who may not come from research or social science backgrounds have an opportunity to participate in a guided research project and to develop new skills. These skills can then be applied in other work.

- Field staff feel a sense of ownership of the research, and a stronger commitment to follow up on what they find during the research period than they would have if asked to follow up on the conclusions which 'outsiders', or people from an exclusively academic background, had developed.

- Since Oxfam and SCF have been working together on the project, there has been an opportunity for close collaboration between these agencies. It means that field staff get an increased understanding of a partner agency's ways of working and thinking, and see further room for cooperation and collaboration.

Deliberately including 'non-programme staff' in the project has also helped to bridge the gap of understanding that can often occur between programmes and administration. It provides valued administrative staff with an opportunity to see and participate in a project that increases their understanding of the community and the problems dealt with by the programme officers. This can serve to improve intra-office communication.

There are also strong arguments for broadening the research teams to include members of other INGOs, LNGOs, or government offices if possible, for the same reasons as listed above. These people may actually be in a position to do something about the results of the research and are also in a strong position to advocate for change among their colleagues.

There are some problems with expanding participation in the LTD process.[19] Thus far no government officials have been invited to participate, as there is uncertainty about how to break down the barriers that would enable them simply to be team members, rather than revered and respected officials. How to undo years of government-service training, which is the polar opposite of a participatory approach, is another obstacle. However, continuing to develop strategies to overcome these obstacles is important. Regardless of their background, researchers need to have some degree of humility and a desire to learn from the participants.

Another important characteristic of the research teams was their gender balance. Within the small-group work, members of the team were encouraged to rotate their positions so that it was not always the woman listening to a women's group, the man doing the introduction, and the field person from SCF facilitating the children's group. This was intended to broaden field staff's experience and also to provide fresh ears to listen to different groups.

The question of who participates in the research team is in many ways also dictated by time. In 1996, the field work was conducted over a period of six days. In 1997, it was over a period of three days, but a further two and a half days were taken in the analysis of the information for the Oxfam reports, and an even longer period for the SCF report. In 1998, in the Wanni and Jaffna, the project took a total of seven days in each location. Even if the project is planned months in advance, it is incredibly difficult to find an entire week in a development worker's calendar to dedicate to this type of work. For the field staff, it is simply blocked out, in the same way as annual planning meetings or team meetings. But in order to expand participation, other agency staff would need to donate a week of their time. This time could possibly be condensed if the numbers of participating field staff were increased, but then other logistical difficulties present themselves. Besides the training, field work, and analysis time, team members should also participate in the planning and action that result from the research; this drastically expands the amount of time that each participant needs to give.

Planning the research in advance and taking the above issues into consideration is the best way to avoid logistical difficulties or a major bias in the data collected. While every research situation will present its own constraints, the points outlined above should cover most of the basic issues that need to be considered.

Summary

- **Training:** most NGO staff have limited practical experience of research and participatory methodologies. They need training, follow-up training with field work, and reinforcement of good practice in the field.

- **Participants:** children can and should participate in research. They offer valuable opinions that need to be included. Ensuring the participation of men and women of all ages, classes, and abilities is essential and needs to be planned for in advance. Participation of the disabled members of the community is also essential; they may require advance notice or specific invitations to attend.

- **Fatigue:** be wary of assessment fatigue in the research population. Research findings should be acted upon. Researchers should not burden an already 'over-questioned' population.

- **Consent:** all major stakeholders, such as local authorities and government, as well as the participants, should give their consent to participation if possible. Confidentiality is also important.

- **Sampling:** LTD findings cannot claim to be fully representative, but they do express trends over time. Random-sample or cluster-sample methods should be used in cases that require full representation.

- **Bias:** bias in the selection of locations and participants, or on the part of researchers because of caste or class background, needs to be recognised and where possible eliminated.

- **Research staff:** using programme and administrative staff on the research teams helps to build their capacity. Expanding the research teams to include partners, partner agencies, and others may build commitment to following up research results.

5 Analysis

When the information has been collected, the project is, in many ways, still only beginning. The critical task of collating a wide variety of qualitative data still needs to be tackled. While this type of research lends itself to the collection of a large variety of data — compared with a more narrowly focused survey technique — the information must still be consolidated into a report format which is easily grasped by a wide audience. At the same time, there needs to be a balance between representation and preserving the diversity of experience. As Johan Pottier (1996) discovered in his examination of internal differentiation among refugee populations in Rwandan refugee camps in Tanzania and (former) Zaire:

The need to disaggregate and contextualise research findings poses a particular problem to anyone attempting to identify views held by the refugees. Yet as a body, refugee communities must never be treated as homogenous.

In 1998, data were collected in the field by three teams in the north, south, and east of the Wanni. In Jaffna two teams collected the information. Each team had a leader whose overall responsibility it was to oversee the process and summarise the information collected on the site-summary form. After the field work had been completed, the entire group met again to report back and analyse the results. The teams in the Wanni and Jaffna met separately to discuss their research, although there were three members of the research teams in 1998 who were involved in both pieces of research. These people had further discussions about the similarities and differences found in the data. Before initiating research, facilitators devised strategies for data analysis and designed site-summary forms in order to expedite the work (Appendix 3).

Participative feedback sessions

It has always been a characteristic of the LTD project to use the research teams to assist with the initial analysis and collation of the data in the form of a feedback session immediately after the field work. There is much to be gained in starting this way. The research teams who know the information best, those who collected it, are directly involved in feeding it back to the author of the report. Also, by structuring the feedback session in a participatory way, the research teams help to analyse what they have found. This helps to demystify the research process for staff who have never before been involved in this type of project. It is also an exercise in developing critical thinking skills, which is a useful capacity-building activity in itself.

In the 1997 and 1998 research, feedback days were held with the research teams immediately after the conclusion of the fieldwork. Each team brought the information they had recorded to the session. A detailed description of the process in 1998 is related here as an example of one method of initial analysis.

How many people?

First, each team was asked to add up the number of participants they had spoken with, classified by age and sex, and to write their totals on one pre-prepared flipchart. In the feedback session, the teams were asked to guess how many participants had actually been consulted. In 1998, in both the Wanni and Jaffna, the teams were surprised to learn how many people had been reached. They had estimated fewer participants.

Situation over the past year

'We can't decide anything, because we don't know what tomorrow will be' (man in Mannar District, 1998)

Each research team was then asked to collate the information that they had gathered during the introductory session and put it all on one piece of flipchart paper. This gave a description of the community and its situation over the previous year. Each team then presented their findings on the situation in the communities. These were then discussed all together, in order to elicit trends in the communities' experiences during the past year. In the discussion of the 1998 research in the Wanni, for example, information about people's increasing difficulties in accessing government services was made apparent. It was clear from the feedback in this session on Jaffna that participants felt that assistance to their communities had stagnated. While they observed the growth of the INGO presence in Jaffna, they did not feel they were being helped. Such observations were then followed up later in the day's discussions.

'Some organisations build two- or three-storey buildings, put up markets, and build AGA offices and spend millions. This is not necessary. For us they don't do anything, and we all keep suffering and die' (man in Jaffna District, 1998)

Community priorities

For all of the groups that they had met, each team was then asked to assign numerical values to the top five problems prioritised by the communities. A simple numbering system was used:

Number 1 problem = five points
Number 2 problem = four points
Number 3 problem = three points
Number 4 problem = two points
Number 5 problem = one point

The totals for the top five problems were calculated within each team and then within the research group as a whole, to establish the overall priorities of the communities. The problems with the highest scores were recognised as the major issues. This set the framework for the next activity.

After the community priorities had been identified, other themes that seemed important to the communities during the fieldwork, but which had not been included in the top rankings, were pinpointed. For example, the conflict and worries about the war and fighting did not feature at the top of many participants' priority lists; however, in their discussions, it had been mentioned in relation to every other problem. As a result, this was noted as a topic for special investigation.

Analysing the top five problems: collating information

Each research team was then asked to record the information about each of the top five problems on one piece of flipchart paper, using information from all of the sites that they had visited. In the Wanni in 1998, for example, the biggest problem was identified as unemployment. Each team looked through their site summaries to see what each individual group of participants had said about unemployment, and their particular coping strategies. This information was recorded on one section of a flipchart sheet. Each site-summary was then examined for responses on people's capacities, and past and future interventions, and the information was recorded until each team had a master sheet of participants' views on employment. Each team completed master sheets for each of the top five problems. Then the group reconvened, and each team's master sheets were discussed and compared with the others in the group. Larger trends and patterns, emerging from the group presentation session, were discussed, and further relevant detail identified. The author of the report then took the sheets and notes from this discussion and made an overall master sheet for each of the top five problems identified in each research area.

During the discussion, the research facilitators were careful to note the frequency with which men, women, or children had brought up a point. Similarities and differences in what women, men, or children said were discussed, and trends were noted. This was the key to recognising the gender differences in the perceptions of the participants.

This method of collating information provided a good overview of the situation that the teams had uncovered, problem by problem, but only focused on the top five issues as prioritised by the communities; the reality of the situation described by participants was much more diverse. Discussions about issues that were not included in the data, but which were identified as themes running through the research, were also noted for the final report.

Further analysis of the data was carried out by the report writers/facilitators after this session, to confirm the trends and look for other patterns emerging from the site-summaries. The research facilitators also discussed the findings with the research teams and individual team members more informally during and after the analysis session. However, most of the major issues and trends had been identified and collated by the group, which saved the writers/facilitators a good deal of time. This process might have revealed more information if the teams had had some time to reflect before the session.

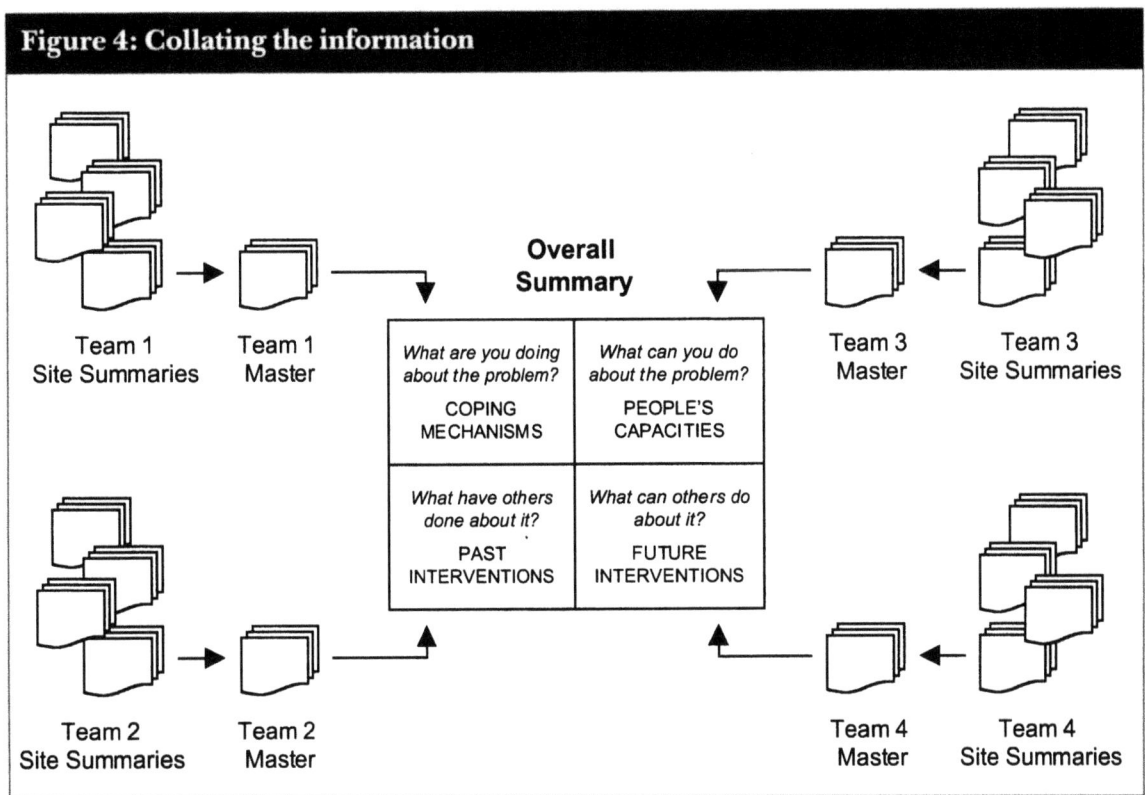

Figure 4: Collating the information

'I suggest that the research teams be given at least half a day in advance of the feedback session to prepare their answers and reflect on the information they gathered. This gives them a chance to digest their ideas and feelings in a structured way before reporting back to the group' (report writer, 1998)

Reflecting on the use of participatory techniques

Towards the end of the analysis day, there was a session to reflect on what each research team and learned about the participatory techniques that had been used. One way of feeding this information back involved each team thinking of a situation in which they had faced a facilitation problem during the fieldwork. They then developed a role-play to show how they had handled the situation. This gave the group an opportunity to look at a problem and to comment on one solution to it. After each role-play, other possible solutions and experiences were discussed. For example, in the Wanni researchers had problems when participants talked simultaneously in answer to questions. In the role-play, the team member handled it by repeating what one person had said and then asking all the other individuals who had spoken to repeat what they had said, one by one. Another suggestion was to try to repeat all the things that the facilitator had heard, and to ask for corrections.

Research teams were also asked to write down the major lessons that they had learned in terms of group facilitation of research and participatory techniques. The results illustrated that there had been a great deal of learning. These lessons were recorded as part of the internal inter-agency reports.

Reviewing methodology and logistics

The teams, who had been intimately involved in the research process for four to five days, were also asked to comment on the research methodology: *'Was it easy to use?' 'Did it bring out useful information?' 'How could the methodology or the recording of the information be improved?'*, etc.

'Sample size should have been increased, location(s) should have (been) selected randomly, attention should have been paid to take a sample resembling the different classes. Process has to be improved to get the maximum participation of the people.' (Jaffna research team, 1998)

The last part of the analysis with the group was a reflection on the logistics and the process as a whole, in order to record what had worked well and what needed to be improved for future years. Questions discussed included: 'Was the research conducted at the right time of year?' 'Were meetings conducted at the right time of day?' 'Was the training as comprehensive as it needed to be?' 'Who should be visited next time?' 'Who should participate in research teams?' 'Did the research take too much time?' 'What could be improved upon the next time the research is done?' These questions provided excellent information on what had gone well and what had gone less well, as well as important tips for the facilitators. These were incorporated into the internal report, and will be used as planning tools for future years' research.

'The time of year for conducting the research was also very good. It is not a major agricultural period, the windy season has started and it is a bit cooler (with no rain) and people were able to spend time with us' (Wanni research team, 1998)

Thoughts about analysis

Getting analysis 'right' is extremely important and also extremely complex. Generally, LTD has employed the strategy of allowing participants' actual statements to do most of the representation. It also attempts to collect high-quality information, sometimes at the expense of quantity. Finally, it never imagines itself to be wholly representative of the IDP population, but rather sees itself as a tool for exposing trends among this population. If these key characteristics are kept in mind, the process of analysis is simplified.

While this type of analysis was satisfactory, it also posed some problems. While the research framework made it relatively easy to detect the trends, it meant losing some of the heterogeneity of experience described by the participants. In the actual written report, therefore, the author frequently returned to the site-summaries in order to review what participants had actually said, and to report back accurately. Recording participants' actual words aided this process, because it conveyed the actual flavour of what they had been trying to say at the time.

For Pottier (1996) the key to maintaining and preserving the diversity of experience is to have a detailed, indeed anthropological understanding of the communities to ensure that nuances of meaning are not lost. A fuller understanding of the anthropological characteristics of Tamil culture might have added depth to the LTD research.[20]

The process of analysis resulted in a range of printed materials, from large comprehensive reports, which are useful for field-based operations as a source of information, to distilled summaries. These summary reports in English, Sinhala, and Tamil are distributed to donors, aid workers, government, the military, civil servants, and the communities themselves as a starting point for discussion. It is therefore extremely important to 'get it right', by accurately identifying the key issues that people are facing, and presenting them in a realistic and interesting way, because the final report often reflects only these issues. Careful analysis is the key to representing people's experiences accurately.

Analysing research findings: a summary

- Field workers are the key to analysis and should be involved in the initial examination of the data at a 'reporting back' session at the conclusion of the field work.

- It is important to link the mechanism for recording the information in the field (the site-summary form) with the data analysis, to keep the process simple.

- Focus the 'reporting back' session and the discussions with field workers on deciding how to record the testimony of the participants in a way that is concise and can be easily summarised in the final report.

6 Outcomes

This chapter considers what the LTD project has been able to achieve. It will examine, at the local level, how the information it produced has changed the Oxfam programme. It will also look at the bigger picture, to see how it has affected inter-agency coordination and the composition of relief packages. It will include discussion of the following topics:

- How gender issues and specific programme recommendations were elicited from the research.
- How a switch to relief items for sustainable livelihoods resulted from the research.
- What has actually been done with the information.

Relief items

A major focus of the project has been to build a better understanding of people's most urgent needs for support. The 1996 report showed that different displaced families had different needs, according to where and how they were living. It also highlighted the need for cooking utensils, an item largely excluded from initial relief packages. Using the report, Oxfam was able to show other agencies involved in relief distributions that cooking utensils should be an essential part of distribution packs. However, because regular cooking utensils are made of metal — which could arouse the suspicions of the military, for fear they would be melted down for bomb construction or for ammunition — locally supplied clay pots and ladles made from coconut trees were procured to assist people in the short term. At the same time, initial coordination mechanisms, used to standardise what was distributed and how distributions were recorded, were established.

In 1997, after the evacuation of the city of Kilinochchi and the areas north of Vavuniya because of military operations, more than 100,000 people were displaced, some families for the third or fourth time. The 1997 report was able to focus on the particular relief needs of these groups. In addition, because Oxfam and SCF were working together for the first time, the information-gathering focused more precisely on children, and as a result new relief needs were identified. Children thought that it was especially important to have hurricane lanterns, for example, to help them to study, but also to dispel their fear of the dark. Oxfam and SCF were thus able to use this information to advocate for the distribution of lanterns to families with children.[21]

Late 1997 and 1998 were relatively quiet, and there was little displacement in comparison with the previous years. It was not surprising, therefore, to see a significant shift in participants' priorities for relief items. In 1998, the Wanni research participants clearly stated that they wanted a move away from relief packages and greater opportunities for employment, so that they could support themselves. They also expressed a need for credit to support their own business ventures. When they expressed a need for relief goods, they wanted items that could improve self-sustainability and reduce dependence on relief. As a result, Oxfam and SCF are working with others to develop relief packages that will address these needs, focusing on providing tools and seeds for agricultural communities, and other items as appropriate. SCF is also considering concentrating its relief interventions primarily on goods for children that will enable them to stay at school.

The following is an illustration of how quickly things can change as military fortunes wax and wane. In early 1999, approximately 30,000 people were displaced in the Wanni as a result of military operations designed to bring 'uncleared' territory under the control of the SLA. As the LTTE-controlled territory in the Wanni shrinks and fewer places are free from shelling or aerial bombing, people's main need has become plastic sheeting. Sheeting enables people to remain mobile and less dependent on weakening relief systems. It can also be easily traded and sold on the open market to provide a ready source of cash for families in an emergency. It is therefore interesting to note that while the MOD has restricted access to nearly all relief items during this displacement, they have also specifically forbidden plastic sheeting from entering the LTTE-controlled areas of the Wanni. So, in some cases, even though the participants have made their preferences clear, it remains impossible to address this need through relief provisions. However, lobbying efforts to change the MOD's decision continue.[22]

Gender issues

One issue examined by the 1996 LTD report was the impact of displacement on people as a function of their previous social position or class. The report argued that middle-class families were perhaps suffering more than their poorer neighbors, because they had lost more in the displacement and therefore found the conditions in the Wanni in the earlier years more difficult. The report also illustrated that, within the socio-economic framework, displaced men have different needs from displaced women.

The LTD project is an excellent way of identifying the relief items to which participants accord the highest priority. Women and men have different priorities, related to their different responsibilities within the household and household economy, and their different personal needs. For example, LTD identified women's need for cloth for menstruation, and the need for private bathing places and (in the initial stages of an emergency) private places to wash menstrual cloth. In response, Oxfam initiated a programme to construct menstruation shelters.[23] Oxfam and SCF also advocated that other agencies should include menstrual cloths in their relief packages. For men the main concern was to acquire shelter materials and tools to help them to support their families. Such findings have provided a basis from which relief organisations can start thinking about improving their relief programmes.

The LTD report highlights the vulnerability of single-headed households in the Wanni, especially those headed by women. LTD tends to focus on widows and their households, because Tamil culture constrains the activities of this particular group.

Early LTD reports suggested that women should be given greater control over food distributions — a finding that is not borne out by later reports. Indeed, allowing men to retain their role as the public face of the family has played an important part in helping them to cope with the situation. What is most important from the perspective of all groups is the need for consultation and participation in projects. Both men and women asked for a stronger voice in the planning of all initiatives, from distributions of food and NFRI items to micro-finance projects.

Coping mechanisms

Over the years the LTD research has included a study of coping mechanisms, using this information to build on the existing mechanisms. However, it was only in the 1998 research that this topic was analysed systematically. The resulting information will be very useful for future programming interventions.

'If we go for work, we lose our education; but we can fill our stomachs' (boy in Mullaitivu District, 1998)

Coping mechanisms, generally speaking, were strongest at the individual and household levels and very weak at the community level. While there were some exceptions to this, and some communities that were more unified than others, this finding generally makes sense in a culture where people ascribe great value to the support of family and neighbours. In the displacement context, where their neighbours may be people whom they consider to be complete strangers, this fact can have a major impact on the efficacy of programming interventions that are community-oriented. Indeed, no project that demands 'community participation' will probably ever get more than free labour, because there is no 'community' to start with. A weak community coping ability also suggests that interim measures will need to focus on the household. Perhaps, most importantly, it suggests that more research on the role of the 'community' in Sri Lankan Tamil society before the war, and how the war has affected it, will be essential for development and rehabilitation planners.

LTD research has also highlighted women's ability to cope with displacement more effectively than men. In many cases this was due to changes in the social fabric that had made women's lives more public. But it also reflected changes in the economic fabric of the society, where regular paid work is almost non-existent, and men's traditional work is no longer relevant or viable. This is illustrated by men's and women's statements about how they have dealt with their problems in the Wanni and Jaffna. Women have simply got to work and done something about the problems. In the context of unemployment, for example, women have initiated petty trading and the production of food goods for sale, in addition to many other new ways of earning income; whereas men often continue to pursue the diminishing prospects of day labour in a highly competitive market. Men have found it harder to break the gender definitions that would allow them to cope better with the situation. This fact suggests that programmes that differentiate between the needs and capabilities of women and men are likely to be the most effective.

It has also become obvious that, in all situations, people's major coping strategy has been to increase their income so that they can reduce their dependence on unreliable and infrequent relief systems, whether provided by government or NGOs. Further research is needed to investigate ways of strengthening income generation in a very limited market. Such research could have a broader application in improving economic conditions in all conflict-affected areas.

People's capacities

'If the government helps us with cement and money, we can build our own latrines' (child in Jaffna District, 1998)

Complementing the findings about coping mechanisms, the research has increased understanding of the participants' perceptions of their own capacities. These lessons need to be applied, in order to provide the best and most appropriate services to the displaced in the Wanni and Jaffna. Understanding the capacities of displaced people or refugees should be a central part of programme planning.

In the Wanni, participants recognised the economic realities of the market. While they would have welcomed the chance of full-time, guaranteed employment by the government that was common in the earlier socialist era in Sri Lanka, they were also aware of the impossibility of that happening. In general they were realistic in their assessment of their own capacities, referring mostly to small-scale agriculture, business, and labour. They emphasised the importance of small-scale interventions, which they could control themselves, to supplement their income or their family's food supply.

Conversely in Jaffna, where participants had returned 'home', there was a strong desire for life to return to normal — for industry, government services, and systems of support and patronage to be reinstated. While participants here saw their capacities largely in terms of small-scale interventions, they also expressed the hope that larger-scale industry and a formal economy would soon return.

In both the Wanni and Jaffna, participants saw their capacities, like their coping mechanism, as being strongest at the individual and family level. The most effective interventions will therefore focus initially on assisting individuals or households. At the same time, the provision of services such as drinking water, irrigation, or schools will need to incorporate community-building initiatives to ensure success. This information about people's capacities has been incorporated into new programme directions and strategies by Oxfam and SCF.

Past interventions

Asking participants to comment on how they had worked with others to solve their problems since displacement was revealing, both for the participants and for the researchers. Participants were asked to describe what had been done to solve specific problems — those prioritised by the community — what had been good about the intervention, and what they felt could have been done more effectively. They had many comments to make.

'NGOs always make promises, but never keep them' (man in Mullaitivu District, 1998)

Participants generally complained that they had been insufficiently consulted on projects. This often led to misunderstandings about the identity of the intended beneficiaries, and the reasons why a particular group received relief. It also led to accusations of favouritism where a perceived benefit was confined solely to certain members of the community, even if they were the poorest.[24] Secondly, the lack of consultation often meant that the project expectations were unclear, and the participants' roles in the project equally unclear. This led projects to fail, especially if they were not closely supervised by the NGO, or where there was little support or encouragement from the implementing agency. In the Wanni, such comments usually referred to LNGOs or INGOs; and in Jaffna they generally related to INGOs or the government.[25]

It became very clear from the participants' comments that NGOs' neglect of projects with communities who had little experience of credit schemes or concepts of community participation was a key factor in their failure. People consistently repeated that they expected and needed more attention from the NGOs in order to move forward. Participants specifically requested a clearer statement of the project's expectations and the role of the implementing agency, and clear guidance from the donor, before and during the project. Oxfam has taken this message to its twenty partners in the north of Sri Lanka and is working with them to plan more effective ways to work in the field. This is a matter that needs further attention.

Future interventions

Participants in both Jaffna and the Wanni have made it abundantly clear over the years of the crisis that they want permanent solutions to their problems. They have seen a lot of superficial and expensive responses that have frequently failed to achieve the intended impact on their lives.

'Meetings, meetings, but no results' (people in Kilinochchi District, 1998)

One obvious solution would be the cessation of hostilities, and this remains an important objective of the displaced. In all years of the research, they have called upon LNGOs and INGOs to use any power and influence available to them to help to end the war. As a result, LTD has informed Oxfam's decisions to give priority to conflict-reduction work. This work focuses on households and communities, aiming to reduce the impact of the conflict on individual families and communities where possible. It has also prompted SCF to think further about its initial analysis of the impact of armed conflict on children. SCF plans to consider the potential for conflict-reduction initiatives in its work.

While participants thought that an end to the conflict would automatically solve many of their daily problems, they also expressed a need for capital and materials to get on with their lives wherever they might find themselves. Participants emphasised the importance of small-scale and household-controlled interventions that could increase their independence of relief systems. While it is unlikely that all the problems in Sri Lanka would end simultaneously with the end of the conflict, the request for a move away from total dependence on relief systems makes sense.

One important conclusion that has come out of this research in the Wanni is the recognition that a better strategy of work with LNGOs needs to be developed. Although in many cases LNGOs are actively working to support people's capacities and strengthen their coping mechanisms, in an almost equal number of cases they are simply responding to political pressure to deal with a perceived need. With research such as LTD supporting their programmes, it will be easier to identify the specific assistance that participants need. Information for LNGOs that includes a code of conduct and clear guidelines for funding of projects needs to be developed and *followed*, as the participants have suggested. Both Oxfam and SCF are developing new strategies to work with LNGOs in the conflict-affected areas and are encouraging partner agencies to do the same. In Jaffna, where LNGOs have less experience of supporting displaced people, there is an opportunity to employ the learning from LTD in the Wanni, to avoid many of the same issues.

Information for advocacy

One of the most important outcomes of the LTD project is the information that it provides. This information can help NGOs to design more appropriate programmes, but equally it serves as a foundation for advocacy work. By presenting the voice of the people to government, donors, embassies, and colleague agencies, Oxfam and SCF can work towards solving problems and improving services and conditions for the displaced. Targeting specific issues, such as the inclusion of a specific item in an NFRI pack, and lobbying the relevant players to change their practice, is one way of doing this. It can also be done by setting out a series of specific recommendations for those seeking to assist the people of the Wanni and Jaffna.

Over the three years, various strategies have been employed for disseminating the research findings. In the first and second years of the report, executive summaries were widely distributed among colleague agencies and coordinating forums, and more informally through government channels. In 1998, a more structured approach to spreading the information was taken. A formal launch of the summary report was staged for key policy makers in the government, donors, partner agencies, and others. In addition, the report was presented to district-level officials and LNGOs in each district where information had been collected. Presentations of the report to the INGO-coordination forums were also given. In each of these forums, discussions were held on how to act on the findings. This was the first step in an advocacy strategy that will entail following up the recommendations more specifically with key players in the relief and development arena.

While some attempts at advocacy have been more successful than others, without the guidance provided by the LTD project, the focus of advocacy work might have been limited to individual or specific issues of which Oxfam and SCF had first-hand experience. With LTD, the participants have made it clear which issues *they* feel are most important, and they have set a clear agenda for advocacy.

Outcomes of the LTD process: a summary

- **Relief:** LTD has identified participants' changing needs for support over the years of the research. This information has enabled Oxfam and SCF to lobby for changes in the composition of relief packages.

- **Gender:** LTD has been able to elicit information about the different relief and development needs of men and women. Special shelter and NFRI needs were recognised for women, and special economic needs for men.

- **Coping mechanisms:** LTD has shown that coping mechanisms are strong at the individual and household level, and weak at the community level. It has also shown that, generally speaking, women's coping mechanisms are stronger than men's.

- **Capacities:** as with coping mechanisms, capacities are strong at an individual and household level. Many capacities for small-scale initiatives in trade, agriculture, and household production were revealed.

- **Past interventions:** projects have failed frequently because of poor communication or inadequate supervision on the part of the implementing body. This illustrates that INGOs need to work much more closely with LNGOs and government on future projects.

- **Future interventions:** projects that promote self-sufficiency and lessen dependence on weak relief systems are those most needed by participants. Small-scale projects that provide access to credit were suggested.

- **Outcomes:** analysis of the results enables better programme planning by humanitarian agencies and provides a basis for advocacy work on issues of importance to the displaced.

7 Lessons learned

While the LTD project is a useful initiative, a number of weaknesses have been identified. The strengths and weakness of the methodology are outlined below, in the hope that lessons can be learned from them and future phases of the project improved.

Strengths of the methodology

Enabling marginalised people to have their say

The great strength of this project is its ability to reflect what displaced people think about their situation. It is not a reiteration of the theories of governments, donors, or aid agencies, but the voice of community members, telling how they feel and offering concrete suggestions for action. This has always been a major focus of the work and as such should remain its centre. While the LTD project has never purported to be representative of the entire population of the Wanni or Jaffna, it has attempted to enable the voices of those who do participate to be heard.

In Sri Lanka it is difficult for INGOs and LNGOs to avoid working with the elite of communities (government agents and village leaders), because the entire system of relief is channelled through them. Humanitarian workers in Sri Lanka often do not know how to conceptualise working outside this system, because they have never done anything else. LTD provides a starting point for putting the focus back where it belongs: in communities, taking advantage of their wisdom and their experience. It does not ignore the elite, but tries to make their voice equal to that of the displaced.

The LTD research has also proved a useful tool for ensuring the participation of children in the larger dialogue about assistance to the displaced. Their voices, which are muted further by virtue of their age, can inform discussions about aid, and about a community's needs and plans for the future.

Flexibility

One of the most useful aspects of this research has been its adaptability: as needs for information change, new players can be brought into the research process, thus creating new opportunities for the voices of ordinary people to be heard.

One such adaptation occurred when the LTD research expanded to 'listen to the returned': those who had returned to the Jaffna peninsula. Oxfam does not currently operate its own programmes in Jaffna and might never have obtained permission to conduct this type of research in the peninsula had it not been for its partnership with SCF. The LTR project made the experience and views of the Jaffna community accessible to the many relief and development players looking for the best ways forward for the people of the peninsula. There are plans to continue the research in the area and possibly to expand the number of participating agencies, in order to increase the first-hand understanding of the situation and to increase the commitment to follow up the findings.

The research framework remains flexible enough to deal with major or minor displacements, to ensure that services reflect people's needs. It was used after displacements in late 1995, late 1996, and mid-1997 in order to assess and evaluate the relief situation. It can continue to serve that purpose as necessary, and it can become a tool for strategic planning, using participants' views as the starting point.

There is interest among humanitarian agencies in Sri Lanka in recording best practice and in studying the situation longitudinally, as one way of measuring impact. While LTD has not attempted to follow specific individuals, it has returned to the same locations in geographically discrete areas to look at the situation of the displaced. As this continues, more information will be gathered to add to the analysis. In the case of the Wanni, where the conditions change annually and sometimes monthly, the LTD project can also provide important benchmarks to assess the development of the situation over time.

Building staff capacity

One of the most useful spin-offs of this research has been its positive contribution to developing field-skills. In the LTD project, staff are trained in participatory methods of data-collection and given the chance to use them in a supervised way, with constructive and immediate feedback. A wider range of staff than usual has been asked to participate, with administrative and technical staff given an opportunity to contribute. Their insights have been very valuable and have in turn given staff members a wider understanding of the overall programme.

The value of involvement in this type of research cannot be underestimated, because it illustrates to staff what 'participation' really means. This is very important when, as the 1996 LTD report pointed out, 'The common understanding and practice of what participation means is to draw on people as a form of labour' (Oxfam 1996). LTD illustrates to field staff that the term 'participation' has other meanings. The techniques introduced and practised during the research period can then be incorporated into regular field work.

At the same time, field staff are hearing the concerns of the communities and are involved, first in analysing the data and then in working on the plans to follow up on this information. This structured activity actually mirrors what they do in their everyday work already, but it makes the steps in the process more explicit. For programme staff who may not have experienced working in this way, it provides useful hands-on training.

New perspectives on monitoring and evaluation

As early as 1997, there were calls in the planning stages for this report to provide feedback on people's perceptions of the relief effort to the INGO and LNGO community. Were expectations being met? Were programmes and specific interventions effective? In many ways the report has done this. In 1998, for example, communities were asked to comment on specific interventions of the past. Their commentary provides a unique and useful baseline for judging our performance as aid agencies.

LTD has been a useful monitoring and evaluation tool for the relief and development operation in Sri Lanka. It measures and describes displaced people's estimation of the overall impact of the operation, and what still needs to be done. It adds an important qualitative analysis to what are traditionally quantitatively biased indicators — *how many wells dug?, how many relief distributions carried out?, how many families resettled?* While it is not a substitute for more detailed analyses, it does provide an overview of the situation. There are so many different actors involved in providing relief and development services that individual evaluations (while important) will not give a sense of the trends over time. What is the impact of agencies' collective actions as far as the displaced people are concerned? Do they feel a difference, detect a change? What do they think the way forward is? LTD can give us a sense of this.

Weaknesses of the methodology

Follow up and advocacy

Even if people's attempts to talk and to listen are successful at the field level, donors, governments and policy makers still have to be convinced. Without the political will to take account of the results of such an exchange, people will be poorly rewarded for giving others the benefit of their time and thoughts. (Slim and Thompson 1993:3)

While there has been useful follow-up of all three LTD reports, the full potential of this project as a tool for advocacy has not yet been realised. Looking at the research process outlined in Figures 1 and 2, it seems that the momentum is low as it swings towards planning and action, but then picks up again in identifying weaknesses/gaps in knowledge. Participants spent a lot of time sharing their concerns with the research team during the LTD project, and it is of paramount importance that action takes place to follow up these concerns.

It can be disheartening to review the recommendations from the previous reports and see how much still needs to be done. While this is only one measure of the success of advocacy, there must also be a recognition that the process of change takes time. Perhaps it is premature to judge the LTD project on three years of work, when advocacy and lobbying on the issues identified three years ago is still continuing, and in some cases is having an impact. However, the process of reviewing and revising plans needs to be improved continually. This is especially important because LTD, as the people's voice, presents such a powerful tool for advocacy and lobbying.

Changing the direction of programmes of the agencies involved, however, let alone other agencies, the government, or other players in the assistance network, is very difficult. Information can be collected and used to inform and shape our own programmes, but that is not enough if we are serious about effecting the changes that participants are asking us to make. How to lobby for and achieve these changes needs more consideration and careful planning. This includes a realistic consideration of the capacity of our organisations to effect change.

Incorporating quantitative data

As early as the planning stages for the 1997 research, there were suggestions that the report should attempt to incorporate quantitative data to strengthen and support its message. This was not done, however, in either the 1997 or the 1998 report.[26] Presenting the report to lobbying targets, especially at the government level, has been identified as an aspect in need of improvement. Exactly how to incorporate quantitative data remains a difficult question. Should the collection of quantitative data be done at the same time as the LTD data collection, thereby extending the length of time that busy field staff already spend on research? Or should the report incorporate existing secondary data, particularly when there are genuine concerns about the accuracy of data that often serve as major points of contention between warring factions? While these questions remain unanswered, it has been noted that the inclusion of quantitative information could help to strengthen the rich qualitative data contained in the report.

Voices — how to represent them?

While enabling marginalised people's voices to be heard is a major strength of the report, how best to represent them is a question that still needs to be answered.[27]

There is always a need to frame research to attract the attention of those in power. Indeed, framing the report so that it will have the most impact, and yet still represent participants' actual words, is in many ways the hardest part of this project. It is not easy to represent myriad voices and a diverse and heterogeneous community in a responsible and realistic way. This is a problem in every year of the research: there were many points that could have been inferred or 'distilled' from the discussions with participants, which were not things that they actually said. In 1998, for example, participants *did* say that they wanted to be self-sufficient, but that when aid packages were necessary — whether food or non-food items — they wanted them to be distributed in a free and fair manner. They *did not* say that the distribution systems needed to be more open and transparent; but that was how the INGO analysts heard it. Each statement in the final report had to be carefully considered and checked, to ensure that it was actually what the participants had said, rather than the outcome of the researchers' own analysis.

In 1998, the strategy for representing the views of the displaced involved using verbatim quotations as often as possible to illustrate what groups of participants had said. While this is recognised as an imperfect method, it does at least acknowledge the central role of the participants in the project. The question of how best to represent participants' voices will continue to be a matter for concern.

Looking to the future — next steps

There are strengths and weaknesses in the LTD project methodology as it has been conducted over the years, and these need to be remembered when considering future phases of the project.

The right to a say

Oxfam GB has adopted 'the right to a say' as a strategic change objective for the whole of its international programme, glossing the term as follows: 'marginalised people, especially the poor, women, ethnic minorities and the disabled [will] have an effective voice in influencing decisions affecting their lives, are able to fulfill their civil and political rights and enjoy equal status with others'. LTD provides a useful tool for enabling marginalised people in conflict situations to have an effective voice.

Need for more research

The LTD project is not a substitute for in-depth research on the situation in Sri Lanka, or anywhere else that it might be employed. The objective is to gain a rapid understanding of a situation and thus to effect change. This cannot replace the need for in-depth, longer-term research, but LTD often highlights areas that need further investigation. As a result of the research in 1998, it has become clear that more information is needed about the cultural changes brought about by the war, the role of the community in Tamil society, and the workings of the food-distribution system. In the absence of detailed information, when decisions need to be made quickly and when there is not always time to consult communities in depth, an LTD-type project can provide guidelines for action. However, the need for further research will always remain.

Taking it back to the communities

'In April 1999, 10 months later, I was based [near a field site] for a short period. One evening I cycled with the driver [into town] to buy fish. As soon as I entered the village, people recognised me and came to see me. One man ... called other people, saying that I had come back to see them again. A group of about 30-40 people gathered and asked what had happened with the report and what we would do about the expressed problems. They also asked when we will come back to do similar activities. They said that people were still talking about the LTD process and that they had tried to look into their own problems but had not succeeded, as the biggest problem was the bombing and shelling' (research facilitator's comments, 1999)

A better way to return information to communities and to continue what has been started with the LTD process could usefully be developed. There is a significant tension, which needs to be resolved, between the expectations that LTD will provide information and that it will stimulate action. The participatory discussion with communities has opened a window of opportunity, but in most cases this window is allowed to close, rather than leading into further participatory and empowering processes. This is partly because of the sheer numbers of communities participating in the research — 25 in the Wanni and 10 in Jaffna. Were Oxfam and SCF to return directly to these communities and continue the participatory process, all other programme work would suffer. Both agencies must decide how to use the momentum generated by these conversations and how to involve the communities in the report and advocacy work while the window is still open.

Expanding participation in the research process

In Sri Lanka, international agencies are often played off against one another in their relations with the MOD and the LTTE. Presenting a united front of opinion, where and when it exists, has proved a more effective strategy for dealing with problems than unilateral advocacy work. Were all international and national agencies involved in the LTD process and committed to following up the results, the research could be a much stronger platform for joint advocacy and action.

Expanding participation in the research by including more agencies — UN, INGO, and LNGO — and government could increase the strength and value of LTD in the long term. The way in which the research is planned — which stakeholders are involved, which questions are asked or omitted, who will be involved in the research — is a key consideration for the future of the research in Sri Lanka. It will also be a consideration in other contexts where the research methodology may be employed.

If a greater number of decision makers and those who implement programmes across organisations could agree research agendas, participate in research teams, and take part in data analysis, it could strengthen the commitment of the aid/government community to follow up issues highlighted by the participants. It could also improve the field practice of those less skilled in using participatory techniques. How this might be done needs to be carefully planned and considered.

Using the research to plan rehabilitation work in Sri Lanka

One potential future use of the LTD project would be as a tool to identify the rehabilitation needs of families and communities. This has already begun in 1998 in Jaffna, by listening to the people who have returned to their homes. In areas where the conflict has stabilised, LTD could provide a useful tool for identifying needs and perhaps initiating programmes that will prevent further conflict from arising. The people in these areas have demonstrated that they have very concrete ideas about how their livelihoods could be rebuilt in a peaceful way.

Lessons learned: a summary

Strengths of the LTD process

- The research project enables the voice of marginalised people to be heard by local and national authorities and by relief agencies.

- The methodology is flexible and can be adapted to an agency's changing needs for information. It can also be used in other contexts, such as planning for rehabilitation or even after natural disasters.

- The training required to conduct the LTD work builds staff capacity in research and participatory techniques.

- This technique can be used to monitor or evaluate an entire programme of relief.

Weaknesses

- The potential of the research for enriching advocacy work is not being fully realised.

- Means must be devised to incorporate quantitative data into the reports, to strengthen the impact of the qualitative information and improve its usefulness as a tool for advocacy.

- Honest and unbiased representation of the voices of the participants is never easy.

- LTD can never replace in-depth analyses of specific issues. More research will always be necessary.

The future of LTD

- The LTD process can support Oxfam's strategic aim of enabling the poor to have a 'right to a say' in their own futures.

- Findings must be reported back to the communities, to continue the participatory process.

- Expanding the research process to include other INGOs, LNGOs, and possibly government representatives could help to strengthen their commitment to following up the findings of the report.

- The LTD methodology can be used for researching the rehabilitation needs of returnees in Sri Lanka and should be used as a planning tool in this regard.

Conclusion

The LTD methodology is a fluid one which is not without imperfections. It is, however, a method that can be employed in situations of natural and man-made disaster to give the voices of those affected more prominence in discussions about relief responses. During a time in social-science research when there are few methods that are sufficiently flexible to be effective in areas affected by conflict or disaster, LTD provides a starting point, one that may have a positive impact on those in need of relief.

This paper has reported on a particular piece of research, unique to the Oxfam and SCF Sri Lanka programmes, that focuses on how to listen to the voice of the displaced, how to incorporate their views into programming, and how to share the displaced people's observations with a wider audience. It has examined the historical background of the conflict and displacement in Sri Lanka and consequently how the research idea was born. It has considered the objectives to which the research aspires, and the methods used to reach these objectives, in the hope that it will prove useful to practitioners who would like to try to replicate the project in their area of work. The paper has also considered the analysis and outcomes of the research with regard to the information that it can provide, as well as what this information-gathering has achieved. Perhaps most importantly, it has reflected on the lessons learned over the years of research and examined what the next steps for the project might be.

This is not a static project, and indeed the Oxfam and SCF Sri Lanka programmes are following up the recommendations of all the reports and considering future research objectives on an on-going basis. This particular text is therefore only a snap-shot of an ever-changing situation.

It is hoped that this description of the LTD process will inspire relief workers and development practitioners to listen more closely to the voices of marginalised people in places where they work. Additionally, it is hoped that the template and discussion of the methodologies outlined here will contribute to the design of similar research methodologies in emergency situations, specific to each cultural context.

Notes

1 This paper does not give a detailed description of the research findings, because the reports are available separately. See Appendix 1 for details of how to obtain copies.

2 This paper cannot summarise the complicated history of the conflict in Sri Lanka adequately and does not attempt to do so, given the other good resources available. Background information is abundant. For a general history of Sri Lanka, see DeSilva (1981). For more detailed analyses of the events that precipitated the war, and have unfolded over its duration, see Aruliah and Aruliah (1993), Kenneth Bush (1993) and Ramachandran (1993) in the special issue of the Canadian journal *Refuge*. For relatively recent reports on how the ethnic conflict has developed, see Nissan (1996). See International Alert (1986), McGowan (1992), Spencer (1990), and US Committee for Refugees (1991) for detailed descriptions of the beginning, and the especially violent early period, of the conflict. For detailed information on the LTTE and other Tamil militant groups see Swamy (1994). Information on human-rights abuses in Jaffna and the beginning of the movement from a Tamil perspective can be found in Hoole et al. (1990).

3 There is a tendency in this paper to refer to the conflict as if the LTTE were the only Tamil paramilitary group. This is not the case. Other Tamil groups such as the Tamil Eelam Liberation Organisation (TELO), the People's Liberation Organisation of Tamil Eelam (PLOTE), and Eelam People's Revolutionary Liberation Front (EPRLF), which are aligned with the SLA, are also parties to the conflict and often targets of LTTE violence. Kenneth Bush (1993) says about their role: 'The fuelling of intra-group antagonism by Colombo and Delhi for short-term, short-sighted political goals contributes to the brutalisation of civilians in the north and east and will inhibit (or at least complicate) movement towards accommodation in any effort to construct a postwar settlement.'

4 The term 'uncleared' refers to areas under the control of the LTTE. 'Cleared' refers to territory under control of the SLA, and 'newly cleared' to territory recently brought under the control of the SLA. One side often controls newly cleared territory in the day and the other by night.

5 Unfortunately a great deal of information about the research process and method used in 1996 and 1997 has been lost, because it was not recorded in detail at the time. The information summarised here comes from the original reports and discussions with the researchers.

6 Excellent sources on focus groups, with information about when to use them, how to facilitate them, and how to analyse the data, can be found in Debus (1986), Greenbaum (1997), Krueger (1988), Morgan (1997), and Morgan and Krueger (1993).

7 In Jaffna in July 1998, with the SLA in control of large parts of the peninsula, checkpoints were frequently encountered. While obtaining permits for INGO vehicle travel was not difficult, travel for national staff through all the points between their homes and the office was time-consuming and sometimes dangerous. As a result, travel to the field could not start before 9:30 am, and all vehicles had to be back at the office no later than 4:00 pm. With travel times of up to an hour (depending on checkpoints), only one session could be reliably scheduled each day.

8 The information was sometimes vague, because not all of the LTR participants had actually been displaced into the Wanni. Some had stayed in their homes, and some were displaced to other places on the peninsula. So while the methodology for gathering this information could have been better, the objectives of the research and the reality of the situation were also at odds.

9 The majority of people in most Tamil communities are literate, and using oral and written techniques proved fairly effective. In a few years' time, however, this may not be the

case, because of the severe disruption to the education of primary-school and secondary-school children. At that point, or in communities that are less literate, strategies such as those outlined in Participatory Rural Appraisal (PRA) and Participatory Learning and Action (PLA) might be more appropriate (see the IIED series on RRA, *PLA Notes*, and Pretty [1995]). Information can also be found on the Internet at the Institute of Development Studies, University of Sussex web page: http://www.ids.ac.uk/ids/ids.html.

10 The questions about past and future interventions may seem unnecessarily top-down and non-participative, as if the research participants had no role in the interventions. They were framed this way for simplicity's sake, as it was important to gather information on the community's interaction with the 'others' in these interventions. Rewording the questions to make them more participatory could be a useful adaptation of the methodology.

11 See Appendix 3 for a copy of the Site Summary reporting format.

12 See Yow (1994) and Morgan (1997) for outlines of some of the starting points that need to be considered in oral history and focus-group research.

13 The research teams stated that caste was no longer an issue in Tamil society. Reading the last detailed anthropological treatises on the issue (Banks 1957 and 1960 and Pfaffenberger 1982 and 1981) would lead one to agree that the role of caste in Tamil culture has changed significantly during the years of the conflict. How it has changed is less clear, and this is a question that needs more research.

14 See *Communicating with Children: Helping Children in Distress*, N. Richman (1993), for a more detailed guide to working with children in conflict areas and for tips on incorporating their participation into research as well as programme activities.

15 Elsa Skjonsberg's (1982) examination of the role of Tamil women in Sri Lanka provides a greater insight into gender issues for Tamil women.

16 In late 1997, Oxfam and SCF teamed up to do a random sample survey of the nutrition of under-fives in the Wanni. The survey was conducted because there were persistent claims of malnutrition, but no reliable data to back the claims. The survey was to be done Wanni-wide, but because of the onset of the heaviest rainy season in years, the teams were able to survey only the western side of the Wanni. This led local government officials to claim that the most severe malnutrition was on the eastern side of the Wanni and to discredit the entire survey as unrepresentative of the situation. This is why geographic coverage rather than population was the criterion for the LTD project.

17 As the team leaders were in many cases expatriates, their presence in the field offered one of the main attractions. While this is not recommended as a strategy for eliciting participation, it needs to be recognised as a component of the work in Sri Lanka.

18 For more information on methodological background, see Nichols (1991) and Pratt and Loizos (1992).

19 The major security concern here is specific to the Sri Lankan context and probably would not be an issue in other countries. There is a concern that the LTTE might prevent researchers from meeting with the community. Involving members of LNGOs, who are often required to report to the LTTE and who lack the protection and support available to local INGO staff, could compromise the ability of Oxfam and SCF to do this type of research.

20 While valuable and informative anthropological sources on Tamil culture exist from the period before the conflict (Banks 1957 and 1960, Pfaffenberger 1982), little has been written about the impact of the conflict on the culture, except in its relation to nationalism (Manogaran and Pfaffenberger 1994, Tambiah 1986, and Wilson 1988). This is hardly surprising, given the restricted access available to international researchers and the restricted voice of local researchers, who dare not be too critical of any political or military group.

21 This was actually an example of successful lobbying, as a result of which the MOD granted a permit for Oxfam to transport an initial batch of hurricane lanterns into the Wanni. However, for reasons that are still unclear, deliveries of these items were stopped by the army in Vavuniya. No further relief shipments of lanterns have been allowed.

22 In part, the MOD restricts plastic sheeting because in the past it has been purchased by the LTTE and used to make sandbags for bunkers and to cover military equipment. So efforts to change the MOD's stance must be complemented by efforts to change LTTE practice.

23 While private places to wash menstrual cloth might normally have been provided by emergency interventions to construct latrines, in northern Sri Lanka this was not the case, as hardly any emergency latrines were constructed during the initial displacement. This was largely due to disagreement about the type of latrine that should be constructed. Local government officials and LNGOs insisted on pour-flush latrines, even when there was a severe shortage of water for drinking and almost no cement available to build them. There were also unresolved issues about caste and class, how the latrines would be shared, and whose responsibility it would be to clean them. Indeed the whole problem of solid-waste disposal in the conflict area needs further research and consideration.

24 In the Wanni, this presents a major problem in terms of programming, because an 'entitlement' mentality is firmly part of the relief system. People who have jobs, incomes, and relative security (compared with others around them) continue to draw whatever they can from the government aid structure because, as displaced people, they feel entitled to aid.

25 In Jaffna, LNGOs were proscribed from working in the local communities until 1999, for fear that the projects would become political or that LNGOs would try to influence people to support a particular Tamil party.

26 In the 1996 Oxfam report, there are some examples of linking qualitative and quantitative data. In the 1997 SCF report, there was one instance of external secondary data linked with the findings of the report. SCF also reported NFRI preference rankings, which were quantitative. Otherwise the data have largely consisted of population statistics and maps.

27 For an excellent overview of many of the issues involved in representing the voice of the 'other', see Sherna Berger Gluck and Daphne Patai's edition of *Women's Words* (1991), in which 13 women contribute to a discussion about voice and the representation of the other in oral history. Other sources for background reading on the issue of 'voice' in writing and research include Alcoff (1991), Clifford and Marcus (1986), and Oakley (1981). Many of the same issues are relevant in the Listening to the Displaced project.

References

Alcoff, L. (1991) 'The problem of speaking for others,' *Cultural Critique* Winter 1991/2: 5-31

Amnesty International (1997–1999) 'Sri Lanka', in *Amnesty International Annual Report*, London: Amnesty International

Anderson, M. (1994) *People Oriented Planning at Work, Using POP to Improve UNHCR Programming: A Practical Tool for Refugee Workers*, Geneva: UNHCR

Anderson, M. (1999) *Do No Harm: How Aid Can Support Peace or War*, London: Lynne Reinner

Anderson, M., A. Howarth, and C. Overholt (1992) *A Framework for People Oriented Planning in Refugee Situations Taking Account of Women, Men and Children*, Geneva: UNHCR

Aruliah, A. S. and A. Aruliah (1993) 'The evolution of the ethnic conflict in Sri Lanka', *Refuge* 13(3): 3–8

Banks, M. (1957) 'The Social Organization of the Jaffna Tamils in Northern Ceylon, with Special Reference to Caste, Kinship and Marriage', Cambridge University Ph.D. Dissertation

Banks, M. (1960) 'Caste in Jaffna' in E. R. Leach (ed.) *Aspects of Caste in South India, Ceylon and Northwest Pakistan*, Cambridge: Cambridge University Press

Burkey, S. (1993) *People First: A Guide to Self-Reliant Participatory Rural Development*, London: Zed Books

Bush, K. D. (1993) 'Reading between the lines: intra-group heterogeneity and conflict in Sri Lanka', *Refuge* 13(3): 15-22

Chambers, R. (1983) *Rural Development: Putting the Last First*, London: Longman

Clifford, J. and G. Marcus (eds.) (1986) *Writing Culture: The Poetics and Politics of Ethnography*, Berkeley: University of California Press

Debus, M. (1986) *Methodological Review: A Handbook for Excellence in Focus Group Research*, Washington: Academy for Educational Development

DeSilva, K. M. (1981) *A History of Sri Lanka*, London: C. Hurst and Company

Fuglerud, O. (1999) *Life on the Outside: The Tamil Diaspora and Long-Distance Nationalism*, London: Pluto Press

Gluck, S.B. and D. Patai (eds.) (1991) *Women's Words: The Feminist Practice of Oral History*, London: Routledge

Greenbaum, T. L. (1993) *The Practical Handbook and Guide to Focus Group Research*, Lexington, MA: Lexington Press

Hoole, R. et al. (1990) *The Broken Palmyra*, Claremont, CA: Sri Lanka Studies Institute

International Alert (1986) 'Emergency — Sri Lanka', London: International Alert

Jok, J. M. (1996) 'Information exchange in the disaster zone: interaction between aid workers and recipients in South Sudan', *Disasters* 20(3): 206–15

Krueger, R. (1988) *A Practical Guide for Applied Research*, Palo Alto CA: Sage Publications

Manogaran, C. and B. Pfaffenberger (eds.) (1994) *The Sri Lankan Tamils: Ethnicity and Identity*, Boulder: Westview Press

McGowan, W. (1992) *Only Man is Vile: The Tragedy of Sri Lanka*, New York: Farrar, Straus, Giroux

Morgan, D. L. (1997) *Focus Groups as Qualitative Research*, London: Sage Publications

Morgan, D. L. and R. Krueger, R. (1993) in D.L. Morgan (ed.) *Successful Focus Groups: Advancing the State of the Art*, London: Sage Publications

Naidoo, J. and P. Schaus (1998) *The Tragedy of Sri Lanka: Ethnic Conflict and Forced Migration*, Canada: Wilfred Laurier University

Ngunjiri, E. (1998) 'Participatory methodologies: double edged swords', *Development in Practice* 8(4): 466–70

Nichols, P. (1991) *Social Survey Methods: A Field Guide for Development Workers*, Oxford: Oxfam

Nissan, E. (1996) *Sri Lanka: A Bitter Harvest*, London: Minority Rights Group

Oakley, A. (1981) 'Interviewing women: a contradiction in terms' in H. Roberts (ed.) *Doing Feminist Research*, London: Routledge

Oxfam (1996) 'Listening to the Displaced: Conversations in the Wanni Region Northern Sri Lanka', Colombo: Oxfam GB

Oxfam (1997) 'Listening in Kilinochchi and Mullaitivu: A Second Series of Interviews in Oxfam Operational Areas of Northern Sri Lanka', Colombo: Oxfam GB

Oxfam and SCF (1998) 'Listening to the Displaced and Listening to the Returned: A Community Study', Colombo: Oxfam GB and SCF (UK)

Oxfam and SCF (1998) 'Listening to the Displaced Wanni: Full Report', Colombo: Oxfam GB and SCF (UK)

Oxfam and SCF (1998) 'Listening to the Returned Jaffna: Full Report', Colombo: Oxfam GB and SCF (UK)

Pfaffenberger, B. (1981) 'The cultural dimension of Tamil separatism in Sri Lanka', *Asian Survey* 21(11):1145–57

Pfaffenberger, B. (1982) *Caste in Tamil Culture: The Religious Foundations of Sudra Domination in Tamil Sri Lanka*, Syracuse: Maxwell School of Foreign and Comparative Studies

PLA Notes (Volumes 22–30) London: International Institute for the Environment and Development

Pottier, J. (1996) 'Why aid agencies need better understanding of the communities they assist: the experience of food aid in Rwandan refugee camps', *Disasters* 20(4): 324–37

Pratt, B and P. Loizos (1992) *Choosing Research Methods: Data Collection for Development Workers*, Oxford: Oxfam

Pretty, J. et. al. (1995) *Participatory Learning and Action: A Trainer's Guide*, London: IIED

Ramachandran, S. (1993) 'The fragmented island: ethnic conflict and the politics of culture in Sri Lanka', *Refuge* 13(3): 9–14

Richman, N. (1993) *Communicating with Children: Helping Children in Distress*, London: SCF

RRA Notes (Volumes 1–21, 1988-1995) London: IIED

Save the Children Fund-UK (1997) 'Listening to the Displaced in Mannar District', Colombo: SCF UK

Seneratne, S.P.F. (1978) 'Economic Development and the Sociological Consultant: a Sri Lankan Experience,' paper for the Social Science Research Council workshop, University of Sussex, 1–2 July

Seneratne, J. P. (1997) *Political Violence in Sri Lanka 1977–1990: Riots, Insurrections, Counterinsurgencies, Foreign Interventions*, Amsterdam: VU University Press

Skjonsberg, E. (1982) *A Special Caste? Tamil Women of Sri Lanka*, London: Zed Press

Slim, H. and P. Thompson (1993) *Listening for a Change, Oral Testimony and Development*, London: Panos.

Spencer, J. (ed.) (1990) *Sri Lanka: History and Roots of Conflict*, London: Routledge

Sphere Project (1998) *Humanitarian Charter and Minimum Standards in Disaster Response'*, Geneva: Sphere Project

Swamy, N. M. R. (1994) *Tigers of Lanka: From Boys to Guerillas*, Delhi: Konark Publications

Tambiah, S. J. (1986) *Sri Lanka: Ethnic Fratricide and the Dismantling of Democracy*, Chicago: University of Chicago Press

US Committee for Refugees (1991) 'Sri Lanka: Island of Refugees', Washington: USCR (prepared by Court Robinson)

Wilson, A. J. (1988) *The Break Up of Sri Lanka: The Sinhalese–Tamil Conflict*, Honolulu: University of Hawaii Press

Appendix 1
How to obtain copies of the research reports

The following reports are available from Oxfam GB in Sri Lanka (230 Park Road, Colombo 05, Sri Lanka, email: office@oxfamsla.slt.lk):

- Listening to the Displaced: Conversations in the Wanni Region Northern Sri Lanka (1996), Oxfam Report

- Listening in Kilinochchi and Mullaitivu: A Second Series of Interviews in Oxfam Operational Areas of Northern Sri Lanka (1997), Oxfam Report

- Listening to the Displaced and Listening to the Returned: A Community Study (1998), Summary Report by Oxfam and SCF (available in English, Tamil, and Sinhala; specify which language is required)

- Listening to the Displaced — Wanni, Full Report (1998) by Oxfam and SCF

The following reports are available from SCF (UK) Sri Lanka Programme (35 Bagatelle Road, Colombo 03, Sri Lanka; email: office@scfsl.childalliance.org)

- Listening to the Displaced in Mannar District (1997), Report by SCF

- Listening to the Returned — Jaffna, Full Report by Oxfam and SCF

Appendix 2
Questions asked in interview groups in 1997

Note: All questioning was in the Tamil language. This list is a translation of questions as asked.

1 Non-food relief items

- Did you receive any non-food relief items?
- If so, what were the items you received?
- Where and when did you receive these items?
- How long were you displaced before receiving relief items?
- From whom did you receive these items?
- Did anyone come to you before or after you were given the items to discuss your needs?
- Were the items that you received useful and adequate?
- Were you notified in advance regarding distribution?
- If so, who gave you the information?
- Were local people from your location included in the distribution process?
- Did anyone discuss the needs of children? The disabled? Of women? Of the elderly?
- If so, was this done before or after distributions?

2 Water

- What are your sources of water?
- How far away?
- Is the water of good quality? / Can you drink it?
- Are there problems regarding access to drinking water?
- Can you get water whenever you need it?
- Who collects water for your house?
- How many hours do you spend each day collecting water?
- Have you had water shortages here?
- If so, what do you do in that situation?
- Have you seen tube-well buckets?
- If so, have you used them?
- Are they acceptable or problematic?

3 Health and issues of gender, youth, and disability

- What is your access to health-care? Distance, frequency of clinics, hospitals, mobile clinics?
- Is there any indigenous health care available locally?
- Have you received assistance or health teaching from Public Health staff (PHMs, RHAs, PHIs, HVs)?
- Do you get assistance or advice from other sources?
- What are the most common diseases in your area?
- Did you suffer from these problems before you arrived here?
- Have you or any members of your immediate family suffered from these problems?
- Are there any groups more affected by health problems than others? Women? Children? Old people?
- Do women meet separately to discuss or deal with health or social problems?
- Are psychological problems a significant factor in this area?
- Are any groups more affected by psychological problems than others?
- Are you aware of any counselling services available in this area?
- Are there disabled people in your location?
- Is there any assistance available for them?
- Is anyone caring for unaccompanied children in your location?
- Are you eating foods you prefer, or using less desirable ones? If alternatives, why?
  Do you engage in home-gardening?
- What proportion of your food comes from markets and what do you produce?

4 Household incomes

a For IDP's:
- What were your major income sources before displacement?
- What are your major sources of income now?
- If different, where did you learn the new skills?
- What are local employment opportunities in your area?
- What is your daily wage now?
- How does this compare with before displacement?
- How much are wages for long-term residents doing the same work?
- What are the earning opportunities for female-headed households in this location?
- What opportunities for women?

- How is cash managed in the household? Men separately, women separately, children separately?
- Do the children work?
- Who has more income opportunities, IDPs or hosts?

b. For hosts:
- How long have you lived in this location?
- How many families live here permanently?
- How do you earn your living here?
- How many displaced families live here?
- Has the economy / health / social relations been affected by the displacements?
- Has your household income been increased or decreased from the time of the displacements?
- Have your vocations / income sources been changed or remained the same?
- Are there any new sources of income available now? If so, what are they?
- Have you sheltered displaced families, yours or those introduced by others?
- Have the displaced people affected water use or agriculture?
- Have they affected education, health care, or other social factors?
- What employment / income sources are there for men, women, children?
- Who has more income opportunities, IDPs or hosts?
- Has your life been changed by the displacements? If so, how?

5 NGOs

- What are the primary problems in this community?
- Are you aware of any organisations assisting with these problems?
- What kind of assistance have you received? When?
- Do you have any suggestions to improve the assistance?

6 Children

a. Questions asked of children:
- What is your place of origin?
- How many times were you displaced?
- How many members in your family?
- Are you going to school?
- How many of your brothers / sisters go to school?
- If not attending, what are the reasons? Access? Financial? Uniforms? Supplies? Other?
- If facilities were available, would it be possible for you to go to school?
- What is the distance from your home to the school?
- How do you get to school?
- Are the school / teachers good?
- Have you been affected by any illnesses?
- At what times do you take your meals?
- What games do you play?
- Do you use the latrine?

b. Questions asked of community leaders
- How many children live in this location?
- How many children are going to school?
- How many children are not attending school?
- Are the schools well equipped and staffed?
- What is the standard of education in local schools following the displacements?
- Have any steps been taken to improve the standards since displacement?
- Have school uniforms, books, supplies been distributed?
- What are the major problems among children at this location?
- What are the common diseases among children in this location?
- (For host villages:) Have you observed any changes regarding your children since the displacements?

7 Demographics

- How many families in this location?
- If displaced, what are your places of origin?
- If local, how long have you lived here?
- If displaced, how many times did you move?
- Are there schools?
- How many children attend?
- If not attending, what are the reasons?
- How is the quality of the school and the teachers?
- Is there a hospital / clinic / mobile clinic?
- If not, what do you do for health care? For childbirth?

Appendix 3
Site Information Recording Sheet

Site Summary

Name of Village: .... Team Leader Name: ....

AGA Division: ....

Population of the immediate community:

Total # of families	# of IDP families	# of permanent residents

Participants in the group:

Total #	# of women	# of men	# of children

Description of the community: How long have they been there, major occupation, living conditions, access to water, access to health care, access to education:

How has the situation changed over the last year: have services improved? how? have they been displaced?

Top ten problems identified by the community:

1. 6.

2. 7.

3. 8.

4. 9.

5. 10.

Problem: Type of group:

What are they doing about it now?	What could they do about it in the future?
What have others done about it?	What could others do about it?

Problem: Type of group:

What are they doing about it now?	What could they do about it in the future?
What have others done about it?	What could others do about it?

Appendix 3

Problem: Type of group:

What are they doing about it now?	What could they do about it in the future?
What have others done about it?	What could others do about it?

Problem: Type of group:

What are they doing about it now?	What could they do about it in the future?
What have others done about it?	What could others do about it?

Problem: Type of group:

What are they doing about it now?	What could they do about it in the future?
What have others done about it?	What could others do about it?

Problem: Type of group:

What are they doing about it now?	What could they do about it in the future?
What have others done about it?	What could others do about it?

Appendix 3

Quotes:

Recommendations:

Other Comments:

Process learning/reflection (refer to handout)
Comments on the context: (position/observation):

Comments on the facilitation (listening, focus, observation, status, children):

Index

access to services 9, 11, 26, 40
action research 15
advocacy 46-7, 49-50
AGA divisions 18-19, 36
age factors 23, 25, 34, 38
agenda setting, participants 21-2, 24
anti-Tamil riots 9-11
armed conflict 7
    children 46, 54n14
    ethnicity *8*, 9-11
    landmines 26, 33
    LTTE 9-11
    research logistics 33
assessment fatigue 35, 38
attention spans, children's groups 29

bias, research 36-7, 38
body language 32
brainstorming 26
Buddhist Sinhalese 9
Burkey, Stan 15, 24
Bush, Kenneth 53n3

capacities, displaced people 45, 47
caste 54n13
Chambers, R. 21, 24, 30, 33
children
    armed conflict 46, 54n14
    drawings 29, 33-4
    education 44, 54n9
    nutrition research 54n16
    participants 29, 33-4, 43, 48
    voice 26
cluster sampling 36
colonialism 9
community: *see* displaced community; host community
confidentiality 35-6, 38
consent 35-6, 38
conversations 24, 26, 32
cooking utensils 43
coping mechanisms
    displaced community 24, 28, 44
    gender 45, 47
    individual/family level 44-5
    unemployment 40
credit access 43, 46

debriefing, research teams 29
development workers, listening skills 24

disabled people 26, 35, 38
displaced community 26
    capacities 45, 47
    coping mechanisms 24, 28, 44, 45, 47
    expectations from projects 45-6
    field staff 33, 49
    gender factors 44, 45, 47
    intervention 44, 45-6
    LNGOs 20
    needs 15, 16, 35-6, 43-4
    NGOs 45
    problems 24, 39-40
    reporting back 51, 52
    Sri Lankan government 11, 44
    voice 20, 24, 52
displacement 10, 15
    emergency status 17-18
    personal experience 14
distribution, humanitarian aid 50
donors 16
drawings 29, 33-4

Edi Bala military operation 19
education 9, 44, 54n9
elites, Sri Lanka 48
employment opportunities 43, 44
English language 29
entitlement mentality 55n24
ethnic conflict *8*, 9-11

facilitation 31-2
    collating information 40
    gender differences 34
    positioning *31*, 32
family support 44
feedback 29, 35, 39, 49
field staff 33, 37, 42, 49
focus groups 22-4, 53n6
food distribution 11, 44

Gandhi, Rajiv *13*
gender factors 23
    displaced community 44, 45, 47
    food distribution 44
    group work 26
    participation 25, 34, 38, 40
    research team 37
    Tamil culture 34, 54n15
    voice 34
Gluck, Sherna Berger 55n27

government officials 16, 37
Grama Sevakas 36
group work 26, 27-8, 29

health services 11
Hindu Tamils 9
history, Sri Lanka 9-11, *13*
host community 24, 35
humanitarian aid 11-14, 15-16, 49
    distribution 44, 50
    donors 16
    government food distribution 11
    Listening to the Displaced 16, 17
    LTTE 14
    MOD permits 13-14, 43-4, 54n21, n22
hurricane lanterns 43, 54n21

identity, regional/ethnic 9
implementation of recommendations 49
Indian Tamils 9
information 46-7
    collation 40, *41*
    collecting 24-9, 49
    need for 20
    recording 28, 61
information-gaps 24
information teams 25
INGOs, local people 50
internally displaced people: *see* displaced community
international aid: *see* humanitarian aid
intervention
    community-oriented 44
    community priorities 45-6
    efficacy 24, 28
    future 46, 47, 54n10
    past 47, 54n10
    small-scale 45
interviews, semi-structured 22-4
IPKF 9, *13*

Jaffna *12*
    community problems 40
    displacement 11, 15
    Listening to the Displaced 15-19, 25, 37, 45
    Listening to the Returned 19, 26, 48
    LNGOs 55n25

Index

resettlement 45
sampling methods 36
SLA 53n7
Sri Lankan government 35
Jaya Sikuru military operation 19
Jok, J. M. 35

Kilinochchi
  Listening to the Displaced 15, 18
  LNGO seed distribution 28
  Oxfam GB 10
  Oxfam/SCF 19, 36, 43
Kumaratunge, Chandrika 11, *13*

landmines 26, 33
latrines 55n23
learning from communities 26
listening process 7, 18, 22–4
listening skills 24, 29, *31*, 32
Listening to the Displaced 16–18, 51
  feedback sessions 39
  information 24–9, 46–7
  Jaffna 15–19, 25, 37, 45
  Kilinochchi 15, 18
  listening skills 29, *31*, 32
  Mannar District 18, 36
  methodology 21–2, 24–30, 36, 41–2
  Mullaitivu 18, 29, 36
  rehabilitation work 51, 52
  reports 42
  research findings 47
  social/economic changes 44–5
  strengths 48–9, 52
  timing of research 25, 36–7, 42
  trends 36, 42
  Wanni 15, 18, 24–5, 36, 37
  weaknesses 49–50, 52
  see also participants
Listening to the Returned 19, 26, 48, 53n8
literacy 53–4n9
LNGOs
  displaced community 20
  information for 46, 47
  Jaffna 55n25
  Listening to the Displaced 16, 51
  LTTE 16
  projects 16
  research team 37
  seed distribution 28
LTTE 53n2
  armed conflict 9–11
  humanitarian aid 14
  Listening to the Displaced 51
  LNGOs 16
  needs of people 35–6
  Oxfam 54n19
  Save the Children Fund 54n19
  Sri Lankan government 13–14
  Wanni 35
  women 34

Mannar 19, 36
Mannar District 18
marginalised people 48, 50, 52
  see also displaced community
media 7, 17
men, displaced 34, 44
  see also gender factors
menstruation shelters 44, 55n23
methodology 21–2, 29–30
  information 24–9, 28, 40, *41*, 49, 61
  participatory techniques 41
  reviewed 41–2
  sampling 36
migration 10
MOD (Ministry of Defence)
  hurricane lanterns 54n21
  Listening to the Displaced 51
  permits 11–12
  plastic sheeting 43–4, 54n22
Morgan, D. L. 23, 31
Mullaitivu 18, 29, 36
Muslims 9

needs
  LTTE 35–6
  for peace 11, 43–4, 46
  perceived/real 15, 16, 43–4
NGOs
  displaced community 45
  Tamil people 35
  training workers 31
  see also INGOs; LNGOs
Ngunjiri, Eliud 26–7
non-food relief items
  composition of packs 46, 47
  exercises 22
  humanitarian aid 11
  needs 43–4
  Oxfam GB 18
nutrition research, children 54n16

observation skills *31*, 32, 33
oral history 55n27
Oxfam GB
  Kilinochchi 11
  LTTE 54n19
  non-food relief items 18
  'right to a say' 50, 52
  see also Listening to the Displaced
Oxfam GB (1996) 22–4, 49, 55n26
Oxfam GB (1997) 16, 22–4, 35, 59–60
Oxfam/SCF collaboration 19, 36, 37, 43, 48, 52

participants 38, 39, 51
  age 23, 25, 34, 38
  agenda setting 21–2, 24
  children 29, 33–4, 38, 43

choosing 25, 35–7
conversations 24, 26
disabled people 26, 35, 38
facilitators *31*, 32
gender 25, 34, 38, 40
numbers 39
own words 29
targeted 17–18, 33, 34
voice 29
Participatory Learning and Action 15
Participatory Rural Appraisal 15, 24, 31, 54n9
Patai, Daphne 55n27
peace, need for 11, 43–4, 46
peace objective 11, 17
People Oriented Planning, UNHCR 15
Plantation Tamils 9
plastic sheeting 43–4, 54n22
policy makers 16
Pottier, Johan 39, 42
power relations 23
prioritising of problems 18, 24, 26–7, 39–40, 61
problem analysis 26
problem-solving 24
projects, displaced community 45–6

quantitative/qualitative data 30, 49, 50, 52, 55n26
questioning skills 22, 32

random sampling 36, 41
recommendations
  following up 22
  implementation 49
refugee populations 39
regional identity 9
rehabilitation work 51, 52
relief agencies: *see* humanitarian aid
reporting back
  community 51, 52
  field workers 42
reports, Listening to the Displaced 42
research
  bias 36–7
  timing for 25, 36–7, 42
research teams 38
  debriefing 29
  feedback 29
  gender factors 37
  information collecting 24–5
  LNGOs 37
  participants 26
  selection 37–8
  training 22, 29, 31–3, 38, 49
resettlement 11, 19, 45
respect 23
'right to a say', Oxfam GB 50, 52
role-play 32, 41

sampling methods 36, 38, 41
Save the Children Fund
    children as participants 33-4
    LTTE 54n19
    research teams 37-8
    see also Oxfam/SCF collaboration
security factors 33, 36
self-sufficiency 43, 45, 47, 50
Seneratne, S. P. F. 30
services, access to 9, 11, 26, 40
shelter material 11
shopping 34
single-headed households 44
Sinhala population 9
SLA 9-11, 11, *13*, 53n7
Slim, H. 16, 24
small-group work 27-8, 29
Sri Lanka
    censorship 11
    elites 48
    ethnicity *8*, 9-11, 18
    government 11, 13-14, 16, 35, 37, 44
    history 9-11, *13*
    humanitarian aid 14
    Oxfam's 'Listening to the Displaced' 7
    provinces/districts *10*
Sri Lanka Tamils 9, 18
status 33, 34
    see also caste

Tamils 9, 11, 18
    caste 54n13
    gender 34, 54n15
    knowledge of 42, 54n20
    language 22
    NGOs 35
    paramilitary groups 53n3
    see also LTTE
target participants 17-18, 33, 34
teenagers, absent 33, 34
Thompson, P. 16, 24
tools/materials 44
training, research team 22, 29, 31-3, 38, 49
travel permits 53n7

uncleared areas 11, 53n4
unemployment 37, 40, 45
UNHCR, People Oriented Planning 15
university quota system 9

voice 55n27
    children 26
    displaced community 20, 24, 52
    gender 34
    host community 24
    marginalised people 48, 50
    participants 29

Wanni 11, *14*
    access to services 40
    entitlement mentality 55n24
    government officials 13
    humanitarian aid 14, 17
    Listening to the Displaced 15, 18, 24-5, 36, 37
    LTTE 35
    participants 25
    unemployment 37, 40
water supplies 11
widows 26, 34, 44
women
    food distribution 44
    household heads 44
    LTTE 34
    menstruation 44, 55n23
    status 34
    widows 26, 34, 44
    see also gender factors

www.ingramcontent.com/pod-product-compliance
Ingram Content Group UK Ltd.
Pitfield, Milton Keynes, MK11 3LW, UK
UKHW050226150426
5217IPUK00023B/1673

9 780855 984373